Flea Market Travel, Treasures & Tips

By Peggy Losey

A story about my life as a Travel Picker.

© 2018 Peggy Losey. All rights reserved, including the right to reproduce this book or portions thereof (including photographs) in any form whatsoever. For information, contact the author/photographer/publisher at www.fleahopper.com

DEDICATION

This book is dedicated to my husband for his love and support and for putting up with my shenanigans that allow me to follow my dreams. It is also dedicated to our daughter whose life path has allowed this journey to unfold.

ACKNOWLEDGEMENTS

I owe a huge debt of gratitude to the many people who have helped me see this book become a reality: Mom and Dad for the values you instilled in me that allow me to appreciate this journey; Phil, for your technological advice; Kathy, Cheryl, Heidi, Judi, Stephanie and Barb for your encouragement and editing assistance; and also to the many friends you will meet in this book. For your love, friendship and many efforts I thank you from the bottom of my heart.

INTRODUCTION

This is *my* story. It is about the events in my life that sparked a passion within me to create a life as a travel picker. The fire that was lit when I was just a child continues to be fueled by new experiences all of the time and roars within me to this day. Anyone who loves flea markets, thrift stores, garage sales, estate sales, travel and an encouraging tale about making lemonade out of lemons, will enjoy this story.

My story continues to evolve through my travels whenever I see a thrift store, a sale sign, or the right salvageable "something" along the roadside - wherever in the world I might happen to be! I hope that you find it an encouraging, inspirational and enjoyable read!

It is my hope that by sharing my story, you will realize that you too can create and live a similar lifestyle of your dreams – should you choose.

As my Dad used to tell me, "Just keep putting one foot in front of the other" and start. Let circumstances, good or bad, happy or sad, guide you. They will create your unique path, very likely much different than anything you could have imagined.

Listen to that small voice inside you saying, "*Do it!*" Embrace the path less taken. Enjoy the journey as much as the destination.

Sit back, relax and enjoy the story of my journey that serendipitously unfolded doing what I love to do most, "picking" for profit through travel.

Table of Contents

HOW IT ALL BEGAN
    Waste Not Want Not
    The Vintage Years
    Curve Balls to Home Runs
    eBay – Lifeline to Our Lifestyle
    A Sale by Any Name - Garage, Estate, Tag, Moving

LEARNING ABOUT ANTIQUES
    On-site Classes
    Online Courses
    Hands-On-Learning
    Print Resources
    Online Searches
    Television Shows
    Great Finds

PICKING – FOR LOVE OR MONEY
    Majolica
    Small Silvers
    Carnival Glass

PICKING UNLIMITED
    Garbage Picking
    Resale Shops
    Flea markets in Europe

FRIENDS AROUND THE WORLD
    Gerda
    Tom
    Colette
    Petra and Andi
    Le-Anne
    Anton and Sandy
    C&C

THE TIMES THEY ARE A CHANGIN'
MY STEADFAST DREAM

HOW IT ALL BEGAN

The dim lighting of the packed, dingy hall revealed nothing more than nervous anticipation. Thick curls of blue cigarette smoke blurred the stacked treasures. Shoulder nudged shoulder to glimpse the goods, without revealing the target. Hopeful owners exchanged secret signs to "mark" prime finds. Silent signals were the language of the night. Anticipation was thicker than the slabs of bologna in the wax-paper-wrapped sandwiches tucked under the arms of brown-baggers waiting it out 'til the bitter end. That's when the box lots go cheap!

These are the crystal clear memories of my first auction experience. I was nine years old!

I was too excited to notice if Dad raised his hand, nodded or yelled "*HERE*", but what a thrill to hear: "Going - going - gone! Sold!" The travel sticker covered blue, hardboard and leather train case was mine, ALL MINE - for a mere fifty cents! My dad had just entered into a binding legal contract to gift to me that beloved train case. That was in the late 1950s.

That childhood event was the precise moment I became a "picker"! That was long before a "picker" was known as someone who discovered "a cheap find" and sold it for profit; certainly long before it was "cool." That day the thrifting spirit became rooted in my soul.

At the ripe old age of nine I could never have imagined what adventure a "picker's life" could include. That single spark of enthusiasm fueled by the naivety of youthful exuberance lit an innate fire for a lifestyle that would later reveal my true calling. At that precise moment I had no conscious awareness that this event would serve as a foundation for a life of adventure taking me across the globe, seeking treasures at flea markets and then reselling them for profit. Years later, I would discover that the profits from reselling could buy a ticket to faraway adventures. There was so much to experience and learn!

Thus began my lifelong passion in search of unknown treasures and adventures. A search for things I didn't know I wanted; things I would fall in love with that would be mine; and things that could potentially be resold for profit.

Waste Not, Want Not

Growing up the daughter of a Depression-era child, I was taught early on the value of being thrifty. You were thankful for what you had and squeezed every ounce of use out of *everything*! Each possession we inherited continued down a chain of usefulness until it was threadbare or had no more working parts. Even then, parts were salvaged for future repurposing.

My Mom performed magic at mealtime with only a few scraps and staples from the pantry. After a hearty meal, leftover chicken carcasses, which most people would discard as garbage, became the base for the best chicken noodle soup you ever tasted! Later, crossing your fingers increased the chance that the coveted long end of the wishbone became your good luck charm. Even that juiceless, brittle scrap kept giving - *hope* that is, to the lucky winner!

"Old-fashioned" recipes were handed down from family members of the "Greatest Generation." Truth be told, I still make many of those "horrible" meals today, as do my children. Chipped beef on toast, rivel soup, Southern pan-fried chicken, old-fashioned, simple meals. Some were more palatable than others! In our home, you ate what was put before you. You cleaned your plate. The television was turned off during meal time. When you were done eating you remained seated with hands folded in your lap until you asked to be excused. Only with Father's approval were you granted permission to leave the table. Manners were instilled by parents who demanded compliance, lest you were invited to "eat in the basement with the dog!"

Every September welcomed the arrival of hand-me-downs as our "new" school clothes. If something could be mended, it was, and we wore it. A year or two after my older sister outgrew her clothing; it was passed down to me. I never questioned this as a child. It was my normal. I thought this was how everyone got "new". Although they were always out-of-date fashions, I didn't know the difference. They were *new* to me!

It should be no surprise then that we would go to auctions to buy "new."

As I now realize the gift of these deeply embedded lessons, I am oh, so grateful, for the values these Saturday night family rituals provided. These ideals paved the path I now embrace and continue to define who I am.

The Vintage Years - A Thrifter Is Born

Fast-forward through my early years of marriage and motherhood and my commitment to being a stay-at-home mom, to the years we now refer to as "vintage." In the early 1990s when our children were all in school I re-entered the workforce as a "working mother."

I was excited to be offered a job as a medical secretary at a regional children's hospital. However, the restrictions of a dress code quickly slapped me into fiscal reality: I needed a blazer, skirt and appropriately coordinating top, nylon stockings and heels. Yikes! Bursting my illusion of sliding effortlessly into my perfectly new work world, I was smacked with the requirement for conformity to wear business attire. No more cut-off blue jeans, T-shirts or jogging suits. I had to be able to put together "an ensemble", and quickly.

I had never envisioned myself in business suits. I recalled several Sunday afternoons of window-shopping in the early years of outdoor malls and realized this wasn't going to be cheap! After years of staying at home raising our children I was ill-prepared for the shock of funds necessary for proper attire to meet my new dress code. What could I do to afford the job of my dreams?

Enter my introduction to thrift stores.

Along my daily route to and from my new job I had noticed a large thrift shop during my drive. It looked like a good place to scope out potential new work "uniforms" AND it was in a neighborhood far from my home. Whew! No one I knew would see me shopping for second hand clothes. Could this resale store serve as the perfect secret haven to initiate my thrifting skills? Immediately reverting to my childhood mind-set of "second-hand-equals-new" I stopped in to see what I could put together for "the look."

After considerable time rummaging through jam-packed racks of donated clothing, I managed to coordinate pieces to pull together a couple of outfits. These could be mixed and matched to make do until my first paycheck could begin to fund a "proper" new wardrobe. Embarrassingly, I inched my cart to the checkout, glancing about to ensure no one I knew was within eyesight. I pasted on a nervous smile and greeted the cashier.

Then, I saw *her*! A woman in the checkout lane next to mine looked like a million bucks! *She* had on a fine designer three-piece business suit, designer heels and fashion accents to envy even the most sophisticated Fifth Avenue couture boutique shoppers. I wanted to look like *her*.

"Why would a woman who could dress like that be in a place like this?" questioned my envious mind. Then the light bulb went on! *This* is where she gets all of *that*!

BAM! Flashing lights inside me charged my spirit anew. Sirens in my brain screamed a new retail reality as a thrifting fire ignited in my gut. It has roared ever since: I *could* be *her*!
My fake grin slowly transformed into an unfamiliar confident smile. Proudly, I presented each statement of my discount fashion savvy to the clerk. I lifted my chin with boosted retail authority and now brazenly looked around for anyone who was witness to my graduate thrifting education. Each acknowledgement of a perfect find from the cashier bolstered my spirit and affirmed my new-found conviction. I *CAN* be *her* and *THIS* is how!

That first thrift store experience revealed the "picker" suppressed deeply within me. It unleashed an insatiable appetite for bargain-hunting that continues sending hunger pangs to my gut today.
That pivotal moment in 1992 was when the picking gods blessed me with free reign. I have never looked back!

I embrace those childhood values taught at my mother's knee. Many would consider the "lemons" of life. To this day I will thrift shop before considering the extravagance of purchasing something new. I've mastered the ease of finding designer labels and fashion trends in the second-hand market. I have also honed my search and negotiation skills to realize some extremely profitable buys. Many inexpensive finds have translated into travel dollars after a quick flip in online marketplaces.

I am now blessed with the ability to pay retail; however, before letting go of my hard earned money, I choose to first consider resale options. When an opportunity allows me to buy resale, I do; the difference between a higher retail price and a bargain resale price is banked and reserved for airfare to visit flea markets around the world and the U.S.

Here is one example of my graduate thrifting success!

> In 2013 my husband and I attended Mardi Gras for the first time. We were privileged to attend the Zulu Ball at the invitation of friends who reside in New Orleans.

> **Zulu**
> *Social Aid & Pleasure Club, Inc.*
>
> *cordially invites you to attend the*
>
> **2013 Coronation Ball**
>
> *of King Cedric George Givens and Queen Monica Veal Givens*
>
> *Friday the 8th of February, two thousand and thirteen*
>
> *6:00 pm ~ 4:00 am*
>
> *Ernest N. Morial Convention Center, Halls G-H-I*
>
> *Attire: Strictly Formal ~ Men: Black Tuxedo ● Women: Floor Length Gown*
> *admission by ticket only*

My ball gown, heels and evening bag were all purchased on eBay. I found perfectly coordinating rhinestone costume jewelry to accessorize my formal attire at a local thrift store. I felt like a million bucks as my husband, travel partner Stephanie and I mingled seamlessly amid the glitzy crowd! No one was any the wiser that my ensemble was a coordination of nothing more than second-hand bargains.

The total original retail value of my ball ensemble was in the range of $650.00 to $800.00. MY cost? A mere $122.00 plus the fun of sourcing it!

We had a marvelous time at the Zulu Ball. The next day I spent my wardrobe savings visiting thrift stores and flea markets in New Orleans. My kind of vacation!

Yes, I *AM* that woman I so envied while embarrassingly making my first purchase at a thrift store so many years ago. Today, I am no longer ashamed to shop "thrift." Actually, I'm quite proud of it!

Curve Balls to Home Runs

When you least expect it, Life throws a curveball you never see coming. You can duck or thrust out your well-oiled glove, catch the reality and get in the game. You become the MVP of circumstances.

That is exactly what I did when our oldest child, our only daughter, fell in love with a man from Europe and announced to her Dad and me that she was moving out on her own.

Had she found a local apartment? Did she and her new love settle on a small starter home in the next city? Not quite! Her journey was to take her on a distant move across the Atlantic Ocean to her new home in Bavaria, Germany!

We blessed her decision, and with lumps in our throats and swelling hearts, wished her life's happiness.

With tears rolling down my face, I stole one last glance as she and her Dad pulled out of our driveway and rounded the corner at the end of our block. She was now out of sight and bravely stepping out of her childhood and into a big, new world. Little did I realize at that same moment a whole new world was opening up for me as well.

It wasn't long before this Momma was leaving to check out her only daughter's new digs. Two months after her big move, I had my first ticket to Europe in hand, ready for *my* maiden flight across "the pond." At their invitation, I got to see for myself my daughter's and her husband's new world and to know that it was going to be OK for *all* of us.

I arrived as scheduled, this time with my dear daughter standing on the opposite side of the customs gate waiting for *me!*

It all seemed so, well - foreign! It didn't take long, though, for me to lull slowly back into my comfort zone when I got my first lesson in German-English translation. I spotted big, bright orange *Floh-Markt* signs dotting the small European villages on the drive from the airport to Heidi's (yes, her name really is Heidi) new home. Instantly, I learned that "flea marketing" was an international sport! Each sign heralded a call to the venue for the local village ritual of trading – used goods for cash!

Just as I knew from garage and estate sale signs at home, these fluorescent signs were the silent barker beckoning all treasure hunters - the universal language of pickers - with date, time and location!

FLOH-
MARKT
Do.-So. 1.-4. Mai
Do. Fr. und So. 10 bis 16 Uhr
Samstag, 8 bis 16 Uhr
Festplatz
Kaufering
Fetzer (0 83 23) 96 74 14

RIESEN
FLOH-
MARKT
Freitag, 28.Dez.
Samstag, 29.Dez.
Oberschwabenhalle
Ravensburg
HEUTE
FLOH-
MARKT

I wasn't immediately positive, but I was fairly certain that my picking hunch was telling me that ADVENTURE was ahead. My pulse quickened! The familiar anticipation of the perfect "*find*" was welcoming me into friendly territory!

Before this inaugural trip to Heidi's new home in far-away Germany, I had longed for a connection to her new home. Little did I realize that it would come so quickly and in the form of my favorite past time – flea marketing. Now, I wondered how ready I was for this familiar but foreign adventure to unfold.

It happened when Heidi and I decided to set out on a short, seven-kilometer car ride so that she could introduce me to retail shopping in Germany. While walking along the brick walkways winding through the city center of Kempten, the nearest "big" city, Heidi and I stumbled upon a small flea market. Was this flea market fate?

As we walked the market end-to-end, the rows of crisply-clothed tables and the familiar sights of cast-off possessions offered by locals to anyone willing to barter, washed over me with a settling familiarity. The heart-tug of my lifelong passion distracted my sadness. A glimmer of acceptance tickled my spirit. A spark of opportunity crept into my soul. That same spark of enthusiasm of that long ago, first "thrift store awakening" softened my raw emotions. A silent transformation was awakening within me.
My step became more secure and my wall of distance began to crumble. I was smitten with the ease of give and take despite the language barrier. My international silence was broken. I was hooked.

Throughout the remaining days of that first visit, Heidi and I visited several other flea markets in neighboring villages and cities. A beam of acceptance cracked through my barrier of discord. I picked up a trinket here, a bracelet there, eventually a suitcase full of "souvenirs"; but more importantly, a whole new world (literally) of opportunity and the revelation of a whole new lifestyle: Travel to Flea!

My most valuable find during that memorable visit was awareness that flea markets could become the tie that binds our newly distant, separate lives. I was right! I would quickly learn that similar to familiar US flea markets, large and small local flea markets of Germany call "diggers" from near and far to discover *their* treasures. A new desire instantly churned within me. All I had to do now was figure out a way to TRANSLATE this new opportunity for adventure into an action plan for future trips across the Atlantic Ocean. Patience and circumstance had just unveiled their response.

Born is the *international* flea market traveler!

I love, love, LOVED my virgin European picking experience. I quickly learned several things: There *are* no language barriers when picking around the world; as long as you can use your fingers to count, you can bargain; all women recycle mismatched kitchen plastic ware; we all try to peddle useless tchotchkes and we all are much more alike than we are different.

This inaugural international experience was just the beginning of a love affair with foreign picking. Since 2002, Heidi's move has allowed my husband and me, and many times my cousin Stephanie, the opportunity to visit many European countries. We try to couple an adventure with each trip to visit her and her growing family. So far we have visited Germany (including Bavaria, old East Germany and the Black Forest), the Czech Republic, France, Switzerland, Austria, Spain, Denmark, Italy and The Netherlands.

We plan many of our trips around both major and small local flea markets, all in the spirit of hunting for treasures that we didn't know we absolutely, positively HAD to own!

A bonus treat is local customs and cultures that we witness along the way. Of even greater value though is the international network of friends that we have established during our travels. You'll meet several of them later on.

The internet and our ever-growing network of global friends has become our "travel guide" for selecting hot spots as starting points for our adventures. We embrace the "smaller, road-less-traveled experience." We rely on our rugged foreign language skills and try them out on unsuspecting and welcoming locals. In turn, they are eager to share their knowledge of the best secret shops and back-alley markets.

Customarily, as the "fraternity of picker-friends" grows, a new brotherhood of friendship is established with a shot or two of the local beverage! Here, the unspoken ritual of membership is sealed with a toast. No translation required! Well, sometimes a little in our instance! When offered a gratis after-meal shot in a small café outside of the famous Clingnancourt Flea Market in Paris we awkwardly imbibed and learned a lesson in French hospitality.

Attempts at local customs often come with a learning curve such as our thoroughly embarrassing acceptance of a gifted after-dinner liqueur.

We were used to meals concluding with potent, burning schnapps shots offered by our friends in Germany. Those are "thrown back" in a single gulp followed by an audible "ahhh", a knock of your elbow on the table, followed by a pound of your fist and then a moment of silence as you feel the burn all the way down to your gut, concluding with a smile of gratitude. Not knowing what this generous restaurant owner had gifted us, we did the same when he brought us each a cordial glass filled with "something red." His gesture implied that we "drink up." Imagine our embarrassment when we threw these back "German-style" and were met with his visible astonished disbelief. What we had just gulped in a single swallow was an after-dinner "dessert" cordial of Chambord meant to be sipped and savored! Using our best but extremely rugged French speaking skills, we apologized and thanked our gracious host for his kind effort to warm our body and spirits as we sought refuge from a cold and rainy day of flea market shopping in his small café on a small back street in Paris.

Large international flea markets that we have enjoyed to date include: Paris, France; Munich, Germany; and the one on Queen's Day (now known as King's Day) in Amsterdam, the Netherlands. Our favorites, however, continue to be the smaller "fleas" in the tiny villages that are hidden in European country sides.

The smallest flea market that Heidi and I found in a very remote village in the foothills of the Bavarian Alps had only one table set up the first time we visited there. This very same flea market was one of the largest "small" flea markets that we have attended in Bavaria.

After my third visit to this annual market in 2017, it maintains its "must-visit" status.
The intrigue of unknown treasures, typically low prices and local lore keep us coming back. No hot dogs and nachos are available at this concession stand. Only pretzels, beer, weisswurst and homemade cakes will be found here!

Whether large or small, the memory of the event's adventure is more valuable than anything we pack in our suitcase

A few memorable finds picked up along the way come to mind. My favorite pick is probably this antique baby mannequin that I carried home as my carry-on luggage in a duffel bag.

She was later purchased from me on eBay as a prop for the movie "Leatherheads". You can tell how long ago I sold her, just look at that description!

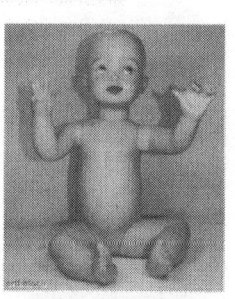

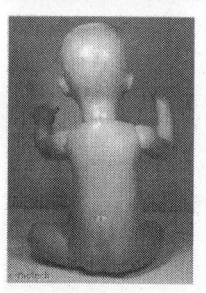

ANTIQUE BABY MANNEQUIN FROM EUROPE

For auction is a gorgeous old mannequin of a toddler child that I purchased at a flea market in Kempten, Germany a few years ago. This darling little gal came across the ocean in my carry-on luggage wrapped in bubble wrap!

I don't know too much about these but did recognize her as a quality item. She is still in very good solid condition. I don't know what to call the composition of her body. It is kind of a "plastery" type of material. She is not "mushy" anywhere. I especially checked her elbows, knees, any place that would bend. All solid!

She does not have her original wig. Only the glue remains from her previous doo! Her lips and nail polish show a bit of wear, but are still very vivid!

She is 29" tall in her seated position. Her head, arms, and legs are jointed and move well.

There is the remanents of an original decal in the middle of her back. I don't know the maker, but she was made in Denmark.

The man that I bought her from told me that she is over 100 years old.

If you are a mannequin collector you will recognize the quality and rarity of this wonderful baby.

Please email me with more questions. I will try to answer them to the best of my ability.

Please note that this item will ship via FedEx home delivery. I have found this service to be the least expensive and safest way for large fragile items to ship. Please email for a shipping quote.

Other favorites include an antique birdcage which we use as décor in our country home in northern Michigan and a pre-WWII civilian work record booklet. These small passport-like government

22

mandated documents were formerly required of German laborers. Each document listed a citizen's profession and work record. Skills were matched with military needs to help sustain the German army during the conflict. In this case, a civilian skill as a tailor translated into sewing wartime uniforms for soldiers.

The greatest reward however, is the experience of roaming amazing venues and just taking it all in observing wares, colors, textures, scents, history, junk, fine antiques, sounds, tastes and people! No history book or documentary can ever compare to the lessons learned from a walk among the treasures.

An example of a history lesson by chance is my first encounter with the edelweiss flower, the "love flower of the Alps."

The lesson and lore of this alluring flower occurred during a side trip to one of my favorite German villages, Oberstdorf. In this resort village rests access to of one of the highest mountain peaks of the German Alps. Via tram we ascended Nebelhorn. Once atop we awed at the expanse of the amazing snow-capped aerial spectacle. From our heavenly vantage point we marveled at the crystal clear view and indescribable majesty of the European Alps of five different countries.

After acclimating to the thinning Alpine atmosphere, we hiked the final few meters up to the mountain peak, reachable only on foot. We found a perfect respite on a grassy patch and claimed it ours for some moments of rest. While sitting quietly beside my daughter and reflecting on the view and all that brought me to this moment, I glanced down, and peeking through the hardened mountaintop clay was the coveted love flower of the mountains, edelweiss. I reached out to pick it to keep as a reminder of this very special moment with my daughter. A quick lesson in local custom and folklore kept me from plucking a souvenir. I was told that it is illegal to pick edelweiss in Germany. I honored local law and tradition and held this memory only in my heart instead of my hand.

According to one legend, a suitor would climb the high mountain peaks to pick an edelweiss bloom to prove love and devotion to his sweetheart, liebling, schatzi. Unfortunately, many a gentleman would tumble over the treacherous mountain peaks en route to complete his mission. Many remained valiant in the attempt but lost their lives. The moral of the story is that edelweiss is a beautiful flower to behold, but only from afar.

My edelweiss flower moment created while alone with my daughter in her new land, our quiet solitude offering moments for each of us to reflect, the incredible beauty of the world from the top of a mountain peak in the Alps all combined to create a whirlwind of emotion and memories for me to cherish forever. On this day the edelweiss flower became my symbol of the reality of loving my adult child from afar.

Upon my return home from this first visit and because of what I learned on the mountain top that day, imagine the *rush* and flood of emotions that surged through me while visiting a local estate sale. I spotted *a most special box*! Placed inconspicuously on the floor underneath a table, below and *out of the* way of the "valuable" items, was a lonely box FULL of carefully pressed and preserved layers of edelweiss blooms in a yellowed and tattered department store gift box. Each flower was carefully pressed and separated by sheets of aged wax paper. Not only did my heart immediately jump to that special moment with my daughter in Oberstdorf, but to the lesson that I had learned about the true meaning of the velvety, romantic edelweiss and the magic it holds to melt a lover's heart. I couldn't help but wonder who the brave and successful lover was and also his lucky lady. I smiled.

I saw something else in this tenderly preserved box of *forbidden mementos* - dollar signs!!!

I listed the individual layers of precious stems on eBay, one at a time. Each sale culled a price tag of no less than twenty five dollars per layer of four flower blooms. They were purchased by buyers in the US and abroad. International purchases included shipping several back to their homeland of Germany. These sales translated into nice profits and ensured a safer way to surprise lovers with the forbidden pluck of an edelweiss bloom! One layer sold for over fifty dollars! This surprising and profitable pick was all thanks to the lesson I learned about the small, velvety flower atop the Nebelhorn mountain peak of the German Alps during my first visit to Oberstdorf. I didn't pick - except at the estate sale!

As much as I would love to have my daughter live down the street, I love knowing that she is happy raising a beautiful family in Bavaria. Yes, I do have to hop on a plane to visit her, which I try to do at least twice a year, but *having* to go to Europe isn't quite a bad thing after all! And, I do get to go to some of the best flea markets in the world with her. She, too, has picked up many tricks of the trade. She keeps her trained eye open for things that she knows are of interest to me during her frequent visits to her local floh markts as well. We now use internet technology available through Google Chat and WhatsApp to communicate real-time to cash in on bargains while she is flea-marketing near her home in Germany! I always have a stash of her fun finds waiting for me each time I arrive.

The apple doesn't fall far from the tree!

eBay - Lifeline to Our Lifestyle

Thank you eBay for the opportunities you provide.

I honestly don't remember what prompted me to look at eBay so early on. Maybe it was my innate retail mentality, my entrepreneurial spirit or just curiosity at the mystique of this new opportunity. I was intrigued by its process and possibilities. Late in 1998, prodded by my "glass half-full" personality, I walked myself through the early process tutorials and listed my first item. That was a vintage lifetime ago, almost twenty years.

To this day, I remain an active, Top-Rated seller on eBay. It is my Plan B. Even the tagline on my business cards, "Selling on eBay since before it was cool" remains as relevant today as when I first penned it many years ago. It is what I plan to do when I soon retire from Corporate America.

Together, with my husband as a willing partner, we have appreciated the value of our eBay business over the years. We have leaned on our eBay success during good times and bad. It has become our virtual ATM. Over the years the cash flow available through our work on eBay has allowed us to sustain the "financial roller coaster" of living in the volatile automotive-industry-reliant State of Michigan during tough economic times. It has allowed us to enjoy extras during the best of times.

While weathering several job losses over the years, we depended on the power of our auctions to see us through. We ramped up our listings to pay bills, buy gas for our cars and even put food on the table. When blessed with full-time employment, we supplement our paychecks with extra eBay part-time income for travel.

To date, we have sold only part-time to earn travel money and help fill in gaps where necessary. It is our plan, as we slide into retirement in the near future, to make the transition from Corporate America to either a full or part-time eBay income, depending on how many trips we choose to take each year. This will allow us to continue the adventure of international travel which has become our lifestyle.

We have always run our eBay business as a legal entity and pay all applicable state and federal taxes on the income generated from our sales. We proudly withstood the scrutiny of an IRS audit one year thanks to detailed record keeping of eBay expenses and transactions. We were able to provide volumes of required purchase and sales records for inspection, much to the amazement of the IRS agents who came knocking on our door. Incidentally, maintaining complete records is an absolute MUST for business-related activities. Where allowable, this could also offer perks for business-associated travel deductions!

In 1998, the eBay selling process and platform was much different than it is today. In those early days we had to take pictures with a film camera, go to the local one-hour photo lab to have them developed, go home, scan the photos, upload the scans and finally list the item with the scanned picture.
Initially, including a picture was optional but a huge advantage. Those early listings with gallery photos next to the title allowed the buyer a visual online shopping experience versus narrative alone. As they say, "a picture is worth a thousand words" and also SALES! More sales typically resulted for those who included pictures. Many people did not want to go through the hassle to include a photo and therefore, their auctions received less visibility and activity. As a result, at that time, it created less competition for us.

Now, including pictures in a listing is a requirement. As you can see, in the "olden days" of eBay the overhead and investment in time was much different than the current process. Today, with a smartphone in hand, it's now possible to list almost instantly by snapping a photo and listing it directly from your mobile device wherever you happen to be. Any item can be listed for sale in a matter of less than a minute with only a few clicks!

eBay became my route for reselling the items I found at thrift stores, flea markets, garage sales, and even curbs on garbage day! In pursuit of stock for my eBay store over the years, I have developed a knack for spotting an item at a low price (or free), snapping it up and listing it for auction to make a profit. I seem to have developed a "sixth sense" that allows me to see "resale potential" in something that others might pass by. It's just a gut instinct that draws me to an item and "speaks" to me. This makes my husband shake his head when he sees me zero in on a "find." He's learned that my hunch is usually spot-on and he now dutifully holds the bags while I negotiate and finalize a deal. A friend of mine who lives in Germany, who you will meet later, says I am like a chicken in a barnyard finding the last kernel of corn! She calls me "Chicken Scratch"!

I am not a high volume seller by today's standards and consider myself only a part time seller. To date, I have sold over four thousand items. I am proud to say that the most valuable commodity that I sell continues to be Excellent Customer Service. That is how I earned and have subsequently kept my sterling reputation while continually selling flea market finds. I buy low, set my starting price with a profit margin I am comfortable with, and let the top bidder win the item, no reserve. I've made what I want to make and the buyer is happy with their purchase price. If he or she wishes to turn around and resell it for more profit, we are both winners!

I do not become emotionally attached to items I buy. Typically, a wonderful travel experience created the opportunity for the buy. I resell the items I buy, bank my profit and move to the next adventure, wherever in the world that might be.

I am constantly on the lookout, *anywhere*, for items to resell, new or used. I shop and buy clearance, closeout, and liquidation in brick and mortar stores (retail arbitrage), online or through a variety of other resale opportunities. Also, I am grateful to have many friends who know what I do and kindly just give me things to sell. My network of generous friends has become one of my greatest sources for inventory.

When selling on eBay, size does not matter. From the tiniest sterling silver nutmeg grinder purchased at an estate sale to a huge five piece set of antique Eastlake furniture and the antique concert harp shown below which I consigned for friends, I have sold them all and shipped locally as well as worldwide!

If there is a buyer, there is a way to get it from Point A to Point B. By welcoming international sales I open my pool of buyers to the widest audience. Whether next door or across the world, the highest bidder wins and the item is shipped by agreed upon and preferred delivery method with the shipping fees usually paid by the buyer.

Once, I delivered a large, bleached antelope skull to a buyer in Amsterdam. His purchase just happened to coincide with my travel agenda to Amsterdam to attend King's Day and the street flea markets on that day. I simply boxed up the skull, claimed the box as one of my free luggage perks with my airline frequent flyer status and it went along as one of my pieces of luggage. I sure wish I could have seen the face of the baggage inspector as *that* suitcase was xrayed! Imagine how pleased the buyer was when we met to complete the transaction in Amsterdam and he learned that I saved him every penny of shipping costs. Imagine how pleased *I* was to get my payment for the item in EUROS to use during my trip!

My main interests still lie in unusual items, antiques, collectibles and anything vintage. These are areas of my greatest knowledge and understanding; items which interest me that I know will typically make a profit through reselling. If something "speaks" to me even if I don't know its history, I will buy it, providing the price is agreeable. I often research identification and selling price range at a later time. It can always be offloaded somewhere if the profit's not there!

A word about prices - it's very common to see resellers on their mobile phones at thrift stores, estate sales and garage sales. They are often checking online prices via barcode and other phone apps to determine resale profitability. I prefer not to do this. I don't feel comfortable doing it and instead, choose to rely on my knowledge and gut instinct. It has been pointed out that I may be "leaving money on the table" for not doing so, but it is the way of sourcing (buying) with which I am most comfortable. Check this out for yourself the next time you're out thrift shopping. Look around you. Do you see other shoppers seemingly "checking" their phones? Many are checking the resale value to determine if there is enough profit in the buy. I do not condone this practice; it is just not for me. I prefer to "fly under the radar" and take my chances. It's served me well so far.

I have also learned to identify niche markets. Women's upscale designer plus-size clothing, new or used, sells well for me. Buying high-end name brands and offering them at affordable prices, along with EXCELLENT customer service, earns customer trust in my reputation. In some instances, they're willing to pay more for this commodity. Therefore, I continue to do well in this market.

Recently, I purchased a high-end designer jacket at a local upscale retail shop, originally priced at $189.00. It was ticketed for markdown to $12.97 and the potential profit margin really pleased me. Imagine my flabbergasted surprise at check-out when the tag scanned at one cent! Yes, one penny! Even the sales clerk was stunned. See how my thrifting skills have advanced? Really, this one was just pure luck but it does make a good story!

```
Store 231          Reg# 4906        Tran# 9960
SALE         Rng: Muntaha Y.

SP PL SPRT:NARROW LEG SHADOW STRI
841078133661                          12.92
Compare At   120.00

SP PL SPRT: PONTE JACQUARD BURNOU
841078135436                           0.01
Compare At   180.00
```

Over the years, picking and the world of online resale has changed significantly. Gone are the days of "list it and instant sale" on eBay. Former strategies have been replaced with a new competition based on search engine algorithms that require a different buying rationale, selling strategy and protocol. New captains at the helm of eBay change frequently and aim to stay relevant in today's online shopping experience as well as keep the stockholders happy. They are seemingly constantly changing processes to increase profits and leave sellers scrambling to keep up with the changes.

If eBay is your selling format it is important to stay current with the platform requirements to stay profitable. The evolved eBay now uses complex algorithms to manipulate search results where the higher search results may be tied to features that require additional fees and additional time to create and promote listings. One example of this is the newer Promoted Listings feature used for price reductions to lure interested buyers. This program adds an additional fee to your seller account when eBay specially promotes items that you select to be included. Doing this provides higher exposure and potentially a better sell-through probability. It also attaches a small additional fee if sold through this program. Participation is optional.

By corporate admission the current target customer in the eBay marketplace is the millennial dollar and lifestyle. It is also widely discussed in social media reselling groups that there is less visibility (thus sales) for small time sellers as eBay seeks to mimic and chase their biggest competition, Amazon.

eBay's efforts to rival that of competitive online retailers bring new rules to sellers hoping to stay viable. To remain competitive in a search, you must pay attention to a plethora of new listing requirements if you want your items to filter to the top. As of this writing, a perfect keyword searchable title and magazine-quality photos on a white background are purported to yield higher search results. The new mantra for search optimization is, "Create titles as if you were doing a google search." Doing this is actually quite easy and does seem to please the eBay gods.

Other recommendations include:
- Write titles with keywords that would match a buyer's Google search entry
- Create promotions and sales
- Create a Facebook business page
- Cross promote on social media platforms like Twitter, Etsy and Instagram
- List frequently
- Enter as much item detail as possible and include crisp photos on either a plain black or white background
- Share your listings on the many Facebook groups to gain more exposure - and don't forget to share others listings too!
- Post on eBay's corporate Facebook page

These all are considerations for every single listing. It can become overwhelming. However, if you choose to "go with the flow" and stay current with platform requirements it's not difficult. You can do it, but it requires close attention to platform changes and requirements, which by the way, are not always easy to unearth. This isn't Pierre Omidyar's eBay anymore!

With today's swing from brick and mortar retail to an online business model, eBay is trying to keep pace with competition and draw more buyers, hence more sales and more profit – gotta keep the stockholders happy. eBay is actually staying on the leading edge of offering a worldwide marketplace that is safe, competitive and also groundbreaking. It is my opinion that they are not only staying competitive in the fierce online marketplace, but also pushing the envelope for that "unique buying/selling experience" available only on their platform. I hope they never lose sight of the fact that eBay offers a unique market and buying experience found nowhere else.

Online reselling is much more popular today than it was when I sold my first item on eBay in 1998. With this change to keep up and cash in on the frenzy, an entire subculture has emerged. I'm uncertain if it is because it's my wheelhouse and I'm so deeply rooted in the culture or if it's widely known outside of the reselling world, but my social media group memberships are flooded with opportunities for education and camaraderie for pickers and online entrepreneurs. Some of this education is free, others carry a price tag.

Yours for the taking on social media, YouTube and eBay, is as much free advice as you can handle. Wide-open virtual classroom opportunities with interactive and scripted tutorials flood the marketplaces. eBay itself offers bi-weekly live radio broadcasts to learn, share tips and tricks as well as a platform to get your questions answered in a live format. They offer a bevy of subject-specific guides and tutorials from well vetted subject matter experts.

Today a myriad of online venues compete with eBay as a selling platform. Craigslist, local Facebook groups, Facebook Marketplace, Etsy, Mercari, Poshmark, Bonanza, Nextdoor – the list goes on and on - are just a few alternatives. It is now possible via YouTube videos and social media to learn about current reseller markets, trends and popular high profit items to flip. These new virtual learning opportunities offer great resources for tips and tricks for both buying and selling. These venues also offer a huge community of like-minded sellers who soon become your network of trusted advisors. One thing for sure, eBay certainly has made a significant impact on the online marketplace that today has burgeoned into a

34

culture of retail arbitrage.

Many very successful online entrepreneur experts share their secrets for successful online buying and selling. They freely share their "hauls" (purchases), often estimating a hopeful selling price. Other experts offer only eBay selling tips. Some are subject matter experts and share expertise about specific categories of items which gives you a new eye when buying. Many have created spin-off streams of income by writing buying-and-selling guides and other partner programs based on volume exposure. Some experts offer their advice for free others require a fee for more in depth knowledge or personalized services.

Facebook groups alone provide a valuable community of like-minded entrepreneurs. Public and private individuals and groups have emerged to teach everything you need to know to excel in this business. Just imagine that there is an entire library on every aspect of business, both live and archived on YouTube and in other groups. A master's level education of information is available through simple online searches.

A very successful strategy that works for me when researching an unfamiliar item is to do a search on Facebook for a group dedicated to that item. Most times I find niche groups who are willing to share their expertise. I used this technique recently and was able to accurately identify a cast iron pan which helped it realize a nice profit when sold. These are but a few of the many ways that you can begin to build your own resource library specific to your interests and needs.

In many entrepreneurial groups and videos you will connect with fellow resellers who love to share their successes, failures, strategies, passions and friendships. These groups include some of the industry's most successful, advice-sharing people you will ever meet, both virtually and in person. They give generously of their time, talent and knowledge while creating virtual worldwide communities. I highly recommend joining one or more of these online communities early on if you are considering online reselling.

Jump aboard whether to privately lurk and learn or jump in right away with full participation.

In spite of many years of reselling online, I continue to learn new things daily. I'll often wind down my day with a YouTube video or a browse through Facebook groups. Keeping eyes and ears open to continual learning not only keeps you current in the industry, but also increases a network of relationships upon which to build a strong business! It is quite easy to use the inspiration found in these virtual communities to propel you to a higher level of enthusiasm and drive necessary to create success.

A word of caution is due here. It's really easy to get caught up in the frenzy and enthusiasm of finding and buying items for which others have realized great profits. It is not uncommon that once a BOLO (be on the lookout for) item has been identified it quickly floods the platform and tanks in value. Dreams of high profits through frequent impulsive buying could also possibly lead you to amass more stock than you could possibly list! Sourcing and buying is much more fun than listing. Don't get caught with rooms full of inventory and no motivation to list nor a market flooded with your "hot" items!

My recommendation is to be selective, listen, learn and start with what you know. Start today! After all, it costs nothing to clean your own closets, basement or garage and take that first step, learn *your* way. Decide if it's the right platform for you. Make your own online resale experience dream come true, one sale at a time.

Having said all of this, do not be discouraged. Do not let the evolution of selling on eBay dissuade you from giving it a try. The actual process to list an item now is *far less* complex than it was in the early days. New folks join the army of millions of eBay sellers daily and realize early success when doing so. Success stories abound. Just like all of us seasoned veterans did, take it one step at a time as you list your first item. The first time you hear the cash register sound that your smart phone makes when you make a sale is all the encouragement you will need to keep at it. One "cha-ching" is all that it takes to get you hooked! I kid you not – immediately upon writing the last two sentences my phone "cha-chinged!" It NEVER gets old! Remember, we were all beginners at one time. Lean on us for help in your new venture.

Volumes of resources have been developed for eBay selling. Therefore, I defer that specific subject to my peers, as the intent of this book is to share my experiences in *search* of items to sell, not "*how* to sell". A list of resources which have proven helpful to me is available upon request. I invite you to search for more information on Google, YouTube or Facebook groups.

There are popular industry conferences to up your game and meet with industry thought leaders and vendors. eBay has revived their annual Seller's Conference, now called eBay Open, after a several year hiatus. It's an enjoyable learning experience with an opportunity to have your voice heard by eBay leaders. This event is more than a typical pep rally. It really is a celebration of eBay sellers. It is chock-full of interactive and educational and listening sessions as well as an opportunity for eBay to say "thank you" to sellers with red-carpet treatment including food, drink and entertainment. It is also a good time to make and meet business colleagues. During keynote speeches you also get first-hand knowledge of upcoming changes to the platform.

There are also other e-commerce buyer and seller conferences offered throughout the year. These include a huge international buyer's trade show inviting buyers to view and purchase acres of goods from around the globe and other smaller conferences specific to a variety of online retail opportunities. Your association with like-minded entrepreneurs at these industry trade shows, conferences and conventions might just provide the enthusiasm that energizes you to aspire to another level. For serious online entrepreneurs the time and money spent one-on-one with industry experts at these destination conferences is well worth the investment. Many of these events are promoted, discussed and exuberantly planned in online social media groups. Check them out. Remember, all travel-related expenses are tax deductible if you run your eBay business as a legal entity!

Even with the ever-changing environment, I remain in this very different selling experience from the one I ventured into in 1998. I still rely on it as a viable marketplace for decent profitability. I ramp up my efforts when I need to pad my wallet or want to take a trip. I sell to an international market and offer quality merchandise. If I buy low enough, even with the higher prices of selling and increased efforts to stay in the top tier of sellers, I am still able to realize enough profit to pay for a trip or two to Europe each year!

My strategy is to continue to buy what I know and trust my instincts as I run across that "diamond in the rough" that speaks to me. I employ as many of the recommended techniques as time allows and list almost daily. While sourcing during travel I put my store "on vacation" with a message that I will be back soon with exciting new finds. I don't sell as much as I did "back in the day," but I'm satisfied with my current results based on the amount of time that I currently dedicate to listing.

I do still plan for that fast-approaching day when I leave Corporate America and sell as much on eBay as necessary to continue our lifestyle, including international travel. One thing is certain; the life I lead today would never be possible without this amazing online marketplace. I've stuck it out over the years, stayed current and rolled with the changes. I continue to respect the opportunity it affords for me to live my dream.

Sales by Any Name - Garage, Estate, Rummage, Tag, Moving

Necessity, the mother of discovery!

In the late 1990s, I experienced breathing difficulties when in malls or other retail establishments that had large inventories of new clothing. Regularly, I became light-headed and dizzy when frequenting these stores. I found myself avoiding shopping in brick and mortar retail stores (mostly malls) because of this.

It was during visits to resale shops that I realized that I did not get the same allergic reaction. When putting two and two together, it made perfect sense to my doctor and me that it was likely the stock in the stores that was causing an allergic sensitivity. Many new and unwashed garments had fabrics that were treated with sizings containing harsh chemicals. I had developed intolerance to the chemicals that are used on new articles of clothing and shipped to our retail stores from foreign shores. When I frequented stores with merchandise treated with these chemicals I had an adverse respiratory reaction to the airborne off-gas chemicals.

When I avoided retail establishments, I was symptom free. As a result I shopped less and less in retail brick and mortar stores where new goods were sold and my turned more to resale shopping. To this day, these off-gases affect my ability to shop in some stores. Now, I simply avoid them as much as possible.

Because the reaction didn't occur in resale shops or other places with lower concentrations of these chemicals (since most of the water-soluble finishes are water soluble and have been removed through laundering), I find shopping enjoyable again. Even more reason for me to frequent thrift and resale shops!

This chemical reaction and my *"ah-ha"* thrift store moment in 1997 were the springboards to discovering opportunities to feed my retail therapy through secondhand sources. Coincidentally, this is the same time that my success on eBay began to flourish.

Enter the wonderful world of garage, estate, tag and moving sales and flea markets!

Early on, I used these sale venues not only to escape the "bad air" of retail, but to find unique items to sell. With only a small investment, I could take a risk and learn along the way while expanding my knowledge of collectibles and antiques and honing my bargaining skills.

I started attending more and more sales and serendipitously began my journey into the antiques world. A couple of very profitable "gut call" purchases at garage sales nudged me to look beyond the limits of print resources to learn about antiques and search for formal educational opportunities. My thirst to learn more about these period collectibles was parched!

The more items I saw at these sales, the more I realized how little I knew about them. I wanted to learn their history. I began purchasing items that "spoke to me." I began to research unfamiliar finds and network with other like-minded friends and subject matter experts.

Sadly, within my circle of resources at that time it became evident to me; with few exceptions, many professional antiques dealers kept their knowledge close to their chests. It was disappointing that most weren't willing to share their expertise. I felt this to be a real disservice to this fading industry since so much could be learned from them. Fortunately, I found those who did share, did so with abandon and also seemed to be very successful! To them I am most grateful.

Next task: find antiques classes!

LEARNING ABOUT ANTIQUES

The more successful I became on eBay, the more I wanted to learn about antiques. Mainly it was to make sure that I was correctly identifying and honestly representing what I was selling. I also wanted to be more knowledgeable in the field while picking.

I naively assumed that there was going to be a glut of formal antique educational resources from which to choose. Wrong! Through the Yellow Pages (remember those?), local newspapers, early internet searches and just plain dumb luck I was able to begin building a scrappy Antique Knowledge library. Each sale, encounter and opportunity had its own story! I continue to add new chapters to my personal antiques and collectibles knowledge bank each time I find something that I have never encountered before. When I purchased an item that was unfamiliar to me, I went into research mode. My ignorance diminished and what I learned through research increased my knowledge for a wide variety of items.

Before I became comfortable talking "antiques," I found it difficult engaging the experts to freely share their wealth of information in meaningful dialogue. I don't know why. Naively, I thought they would embrace the opportunity to welcome new enthusiasts so as to pass along information to future generations. Sadly, in my experience this wasn't the case. When my attempts to engage in conversation fell flat, I thanked the expert and moved on.

Perhaps they declined sharing their "wisdom and *secrets"* because they thought I wanted to realize a profit from their expertise? Or, rather than share their knowledge, they preferred that I just *buy* from them? Could the explanation be that it takes years to learn from a "hands-on" experience (which it does) and thus be much too complex for a brief conversation?

Perhaps a few were embittered as their previously lucrative antiques businesses began fading from prosperity, now prey to new online realities? Or was my approach all wrong; had I breached an unknown industry "code?"

I share this with full knowledge that my experience is not a popular opinion and could result in disagreement from my readers. It is based on my actual perception and experiences at the time. It's still a mystery to me. I share my personal experience with the hope that it was indeed unintentional and just my nervous perception, in an effort to help others who may wish to break the ice and engage in dialogue with experts.

Yes, it was difficult for me to find people who would share their expertise when I was a "newbie." That is, until I began my first in-person, classroom-style lessons and met my first mentor!

On-Site Classes

Through a local newspaper I found an antiques mall twenty-six miles from my house that offered a six-week course. I signed up immediately. The course was taught by an extremely personable and knowledgeable expert who used actual antique examples from the stocked shelves of the brick and mortar mall in which the class was held. He also provided the class with a detailed course syllabus and weekly course reference materials. To this day, I reference the materials from this class series.

I still fondly carry mental images of John's vivid story telling lectures. Through historical story telling he took you back in time to the events of the era of the item being discussed. I swear I could feel the arid conditions of the post-industrial revolution factories where transferware was being mass produced for the first time. I felt like I was elbow-to-elbow with the workers as they smoothed the transfers onto the molded forms in hot dusty factories. His narration of the how items were created was complete with factual historical reference. His realistic historical approach lit a new fire in me to begin reading history books anew! Why was it not so fascinating in grade school?

Sadly, the year following this class, the antiques mall closed its doors. It became a victim of the decline of the antiques mall industry and the closing of many brick and mortar antique shops. I was not about to give up hope of continuing to learn from such an amazing expert. There had to be another venue where we could continue our learning.

I inquired about renting space at our local community center and they approved. I asked John if he would come to *my* community. He agreed! We got the word out and many of his loyal followers made the trek to "my neck of the woods" to continue our learning and comradery. We brought in examples from our personal collections for "show and tell" of the weekly topic, as we no longer had mall inventory to use as teaching examples. We shared, we listened, we learned, we loved it!

It was another amazing course series and a wonderful sharing experience by participants of all antiques educational levels. John brought in other subject matter experts and we learned about dolls, books, glassware, porcelain, china, furniture and so much more. It was also the perfect opportunity for an entry level person to learn "the basics" from industry experts in a friendly environment where each participant could contribute at their own knowledge comfort level.

I was mostly a sponge! From this non-threatening experience I learned a lot about how to research antiques, not so much item specifics, but research techniques. I also learned to use all of my senses to help identify many items. This has proven to be the most valuable learning tool I have ever gleaned from this fascinating industry!

Take away
- Check local community centers, antique shops or malls, local libraries etc. for courses that might be available in your area. Or, if you have an antique-loving friend, start your own group and just share! I have recently learned about the popularity of Meetup groups. Look into those and cast your nets.
- Try to get a local Facebook Antique Group started. Through face-to-face and internet networking your group will grow in no time.
- Gather like-minded friends and create a virtual group using Skype technology. This can afford the opportunity for real- time international participation.

Online Courses

There are now several online courses available. Some offer certificates for successful completion, such as the course available from Asheford Institute of Antiques. Some are affiliated through colleges and/or universities and are "for credit" college courses. Some are available through blogs and/or antiquing websites.

Though not a formal courses, you can now access the power of YouTube online for a gold-mine of free material including video. These are often presented by subject matter experts. Most of these YouTube publications are recorded but if you're lucky enough to land upon one that is live they usually offer a chat feature for real-time Q&A. If you subscribe to the YouTube channel you will get notification of when the shows will be broadcast live. It's a great way to be able to ask questions real time.

I find a Facebook group for just about any antique niche there is. I subscribe to many. All you have to do it put the name of the niche you are searching for in the Facebook search field and add the word "group". It will bring up related search results. Browse the groups that interest you and click their "join" button. Once approved you can lurk or jump right in and share. It usually costs nothing to join. For some there is a small membership fee. Try the free ones first and then when you're ready for a deeper dive, sign up for the paid groups.

Educational opportunities increase almost daily and can be found through simple online searches. Pricing for these courses range from free, to some costing in excess of one thousand dollars. Some also require onsite participation.

It makes me so happy that learning about antiques seems to be more open and friendly these days.

> **Take away**
> - This may be a great way to gain early knowledge. Online search engines can offer many self-paced courses. However, the major drawback here is the lack of that tactile experience of not being able to hold an object in your hands.
> - As mentioned above, engaging one's senses is an invaluable field tool when exploring antiques.

I did choose to add an online certification program to supplement my classroom and field learning experiences. Those program materials quickly became valuable resources then and now as I continue my lifelong learning in this industry. I suggest you subscribe to less expensive or free courses/programs initially and continue learning all you can from them. Once you are ready for a more in depth learning experience, consider the courses requiring a fee and certification programs.

A word of caution: be diligent and confirm the credentials of the teaching resources.

Hands-On-Learning

I can't emphasize this enough; there is no substitute for being able to engage your senses when learning about antiques and collectibles.

From our first class in Antiques 101, where each student was able to handle those precious antiques to feel weight, quality, texture, etc., our teacher taught us the value of using all five senses when evaluating antiques.

Today I apply this lesson frequently. Tactile examination answers so many questions that simply cannot be discovered by written word or pictures. Sometimes the odor, or yes, the taste of the composition of an item can reveal a lot. Even something as simple as a side-by-side visual comparison of two like objects quickly reveals age vs. reproduction.

Much of my learning has come from finding unique items which I know nothing about and taking them home for identification. It's really quite easy to do once you learn a few basic search techniques.

Take away
- Pick up two similar objects and hold them in your hands.
- Feel the texture, the weight; note the composition.
- Smell it.
- Look at the color. Learn through your senses first to identify what you are holding in your hands, and then begin an online search. If you find a pretty blue bowl, pick it up, feel it, rub your fingers around the edges. Make note of weight, thickness, mold seams and back stamps or lack thereof. Does it have an odor? Can you see through it? Look at the design.
- Jot down your impressions.

- Put keywords of some of your findings into a Google image search or a picture for a reverse image search and see what online images pop up. Click on your selected picture. You may get lucky and identify the item on your first try. It might just be what you're holding in your hand! If not, search for a similar item and click on it. This could lead to something similar which may lead you to your item.
- Post a picture of the item on your favorite Facebook collectibles group. Often experts in the group can acclaim or deny your hunch.
- Take a chance, tumble down that rabbit hole! It's fun and that's how you add to your antiques knowledge bank.

Print Sources

Printed reference materials are available everywhere! There is a printed reference book for just about every antique object that you might want to identify.

I have been successful in building a personal print reference library mostly from garage, estate and moving sales. Whenever I see a reference book at a sale, whether or not it's something that interests me (and the price seems reasonable), I'll purchase it. Due to the popularity of online searches, reference books are now very inexpensive from Amazon and eBay. Should you prefer to zero in on a specific subject to master, this is a very quick way to build your library at a relatively inexpensive price.

My personal all-time favorite "reference book gold-mine" occurred when I happened upon a moving sale at the home of a former antiques appraiser for a high-end, well-known auction house. At her sale I purchased every single book displayed in her collection for $1.00 each! Four *huge* boxes totaling approximately seventy-five books!

I was so excited about my initial purchases that, after driving away, I decided to return and ask if there were any other books which weren't included in her sale. The woman was so impressed that I was interested enough to return and inquire, that she brought out seven more books, all at that same selling price of $1.00 each! These were books she'd planned on keeping but reconsidered when someone as passionate about the industry as she was showed an intense interest.

I continue to add to my reference library one book at a time. I use my books ALL of the time. There is a plethora of online images to peruse but sometimes it's just holding that book in your hands and flipping through the pages that connects you to a collection and, if you're lucky, ends your search.

Picking *secret* --- If you don't see something that you want when attending garage sales, ask! The seller just might have what you're looking for. Plus, being in a selling mood for additional garage sale profits could motivate a seller to run back into the house and get it for you! I do this often and bag a lot of great finds that no one else laid eyes on, just because I asked.

Take away
- Build your reference library one book or pamphlet at a time. You will use it often whether for identification or just interesting reading.
- Don't just look at the pictures to find like items as I did, initially. Read the contents, too! That's where the history is and you'll learn facts which will help you in future picks! Thank you John for teaching me this!

Online Searches

One word, no, maybe six: eBay and Google "completed items" searches.

I always start my searches using the eBay *completed listings* search feature. I start with basic descriptive words unless I know the manufacturer. Then I'll look at the gallery photos to see if I can spot my item. If so, BINGO! Done! Identified!

Next, I look up the price range that similar items have sold for, pricing mine near or over the highest selling price. Why do I price mine near or at the top of the price range? Because my excellent feedback rating, plus almost four thousand items sold, equals a trusted seller who can command a higher price. This is another reminder where excellent customer service has its rewards.

If I'm unsuccessful with my initial search, I repeat the procedure cited earlier in a Google image search. Clicking through links provided from my search results can result in related websites, manufacturer's catalogs, etc. Complete manufacturer's catalogs are great references and produce precise identification many times. This information can be used when creating an eBay listing and gives your listing referenceable credibility. If you have a picture of the item you are searching for you can also do a Google "reverse image" search using just a photo. There are really so many tools now to assist you with identifying unknown objects.

Replacements.com is also a good online reference site for china, glassware and silverware. Use their search tools and descriptions to narrow your search. Be sure to click on the images tool on the left hand side of your search results to see pictures. It's much easier in case you don't have a clue as to a pattern or manufacturer name.

Take away

- Use Google image or reverse image searches if your eBay completed listings search yields no results.
- If you are multilingual and know something comes from another country, bonus! Your online search may be in a native language that you can read or understand. Often there is a "translate" button on sites that will allow you to read in your preferred language. If not, use similar root word association to try to piece together an identity. There is also the option for using an online translator where you enter the word or phrase you want to translate and it is automatically

translated to your preferred language. I can semi-read German. Many times I will go to the German eBay or Amazon site for information on an item that I think may be found there. If you are multilingual, employ those skills and market your services by assisting other buyers and sellers!

Let's give it a try. Using this photo, try to identify any of the items shown below. Since you can't hold these in your hands, try to use a google search using descriptive words.

Or, try this one.

50

Television Shows

When I first began *junkin'*, I would get up at 5:00 AM to watch a show on BBC Television called, *"Cash in The Attic."* It was a great way to learn as experts described items they found digging around in the attics of homes in the UK.

A forgotten item, usually an antique, would be uncovered and a highly detailed description as well as an approximate resale value would follow. These descriptions were often shared in the same historical knowledge format that I so loved learning from when taking my antiques course. It made much more sense and aided my retention of understanding an era or process.

Sadly, the production and reruns of this show have ended. I have searched for archived episodes and have yet to find them. If you know where I might be able to view them, please let me know. I would love to watch them all again!

Weep not. America has gotten into the treasure hunting business and there are new opportunities to obtain a passive antiques education. Cable TV channels are inundated now with buy-value-sell television shows like "Antiques Roadshow", "Pawn Stars", "American Pickers", "Auction Hunters", "Storage Wars", etc. The list of these types of shows seems to multiply each season not only in the US but also in Europe.

During my frequent visits to Germany I am happy to watch similar regional shows. In this particular show folks bring in antiques they want to sell. An appraiser gives them a ballpark value and then the item is auctioned to a panel of four collectors. Highest bidder wins the item. It's a new spin on a familiar process. The thrill of learning, appraising and auctions all rolled into one show. While attending a Bavarian flea market in Fussen this past summer I was privileged to meet one of the hosts when I stopped in at his booth. He is as lively in person as he is on the show. The name of the show is Bares Fuer Rares. Google it! Click on it and watch online. Even if you don't understand German you will enjoy watching and probably understand the action. Trading is an international passion.

Many shows now target the popular growing flipping market. Look beyond the staged drama of the participants and you can learn new things with each episode. Personally, I don't put a lot of credibility in the values often suggested on many of the items in these shows. It is my opinion that the value is often inflated for the "WOW" factor and to appease an audience. These shows do, however, still offer an entertaining way to learn from the industry experts that are often consulted.

If there are any entrepreneurs reading this, please get in touch. I have a fun idea for a related show with a twist, but it's uniquely different!

Take away
- You can turn your leisure or "couch potato" time into a classroom experience.
- There is a lot to be learned from these treasure hunting shows, including selling venues, suggested price ranges and an ability to identify items that you might see in your travels.
- A word of caution: Take the market value stated during these shows for entertainment value only. Item prices on these shows can be hugely inflated over an actual selling price.
- Use all resources at your disposal to determine a starting price for your selling venue. Pricing across platforms varies greatly. Check out your platform to realize the greatest profit.
- I always use the eBay completed listings tool and then check the number of like items available for sale when determining my starting price on eBay. Supply and demand, plus my seller reputation in my chosen platform usually yields my highest possible return.

Great Finds
Amass your inventory one item at a time. See it. Like it. Got a hunch? If you like the price, go for it!

Over the years that I have been treasure hunting at garage sales, estate sales and flea markets I have continued to hone my picking skills as my knowledge increases and the market changes. It has only been through a lot of mistake buys that I have learned which items may or may not be profitable and yet, I'm still not always correct. You must also keep in mind vulnerable fluctuations of market trends and values.

In the U.S. we are really fortunate to have our unique garage sale culture. It allows us unlimited opportunities to apply our skills without a large cash outlay. It makes many of my international friends and colleagues jealous! However, in my international travels I am seeing more and more "garage sale" type selling in Europe. The photo on the top is a garage sale that I attended on the Danish island of Bornholm. The photo on the bottom is one I attended in Bavaria. Yep, made purchases at both of them!

Best practices that I find yield good results include: pick up items one at a time; research that item; list it for resale and see what your results are. Each sale feeds the frenzy to continue a new search for another similar profitable find. As your profits increase you will find yourself seeking out items of greater value. Your knowledge increases with your research and thus the items you purchase and offer for resale can be of higher quality and value and your sales will increase. You will soon find yourself a more discernable buyer able to filter your purchases and realize larger profits. Sometimes you may even find a diamond in the rough and get it for a bargain price and later find out that neither seller nor buyer was aware of the value! Such was the case for an antique pin dish. I bought it at a flea market in Germany for two euros. I sold it for over $300.

Here are examples of a few more profitable finds that we have realized over the years.

- $10.00 investment in old Majolica dishes - $1,400.00 sale
- Inherited glass minnow trap - $300.00 sale
- $30.00 sterling silver nutmeg grater - $330.00 sale
- $2.00 bag that included this pair of old Bakelite dice - $261.00 sale

- 20 euro for a vintage gold watch - 150 euros ($180.00 USD). This never made it to eBay but was sold through a Facebook group within days of purchase. Purchased, sold and shipped during a recent trip while abroad.

Take away
- Trust your instinct. If something speaks to you and it's within your price range, grab it and give it a try. If it doesn't work out, you can always donate it back to a non-profit resale shop and get a tax write off receipt (well, that was before the new tax law) or add to your own garage sale inventory!
- Walk past most things marked "Made in China" or "Limited Edition". There are thousands of mass-produced, home shopping collector items virtually everywhere. Just because something is marked "Limited Edition" doesn't mean that it's valuable. Too many were mass produced.
- When starting out, try to stick with what you know. There are occasional big hits are out there! Trust your gut if the risk is not too high and just go for it. Leave no regrets!

PICKING - FOR LOVE AND MONEY

When I first began searching for items to sell on eBay, I didn't realize that what I called "a fun way to spend a Saturday" had a "formal" name called *picking*. What I learned quite quickly is that once people respect your "eye", they are quick to request that you "keep an eye out" for a unique piece or two for them!

As mentioned earlier, there are many TV shows today that demonstrate several different ways to pick. You can pick just about anywhere: at garage sales, estate sales, auctions, storage auctions, even curbside on junk day! Opportunities are everywhere to suit your budget, expertise and adventure.

My picking began innocently as an extension of my passion for auctions and thrift shopping, developing into an incessant search for any diamond in the rough. Early haphazard, "gold-mine finds" at local garage and estate sales netted some very profitable results. Each one sparked a fire for bigger and better finds. Many times, as I have mentioned, items passed over by "experts", for some reason "spoke" to me. I listened to my gut feeling and risked the purchase.

Here are a couple of my most profitable and fun finds, all purchased rather naively.

- **Majolica**
  I acquired a pearl of wisdom many years ago while watching the aforementioned BBC TV show, "Cash in the Attic". It paid off handsomely after following a hunch and it resulted in finding my first jackpot pick. Even today as I continue to pick in the US and Europe, what I learned many years ago from this show proves helpful.

  Several episodes of "Cash in the Attic" featured examples of Majolica pottery which is common in Europe. Although my daughter and I noticed many pieces at European flea markets and recognized the style, I really knew nothing other than "the look" and associated name. I didn't know how to identify Majolica or if something had to be marked "Majolica" to be identified as such.

A stop at a local garage sale on my way to work one day became my chance encounter for the identification of, value of and hands-on exposure to this pottery. The item for sale was a boxed lot of fifteen pieces of what looked to me to be Majolica. The asking price was ten dollars for all fifteen pieces.

My dilemma: Some pottery pieces had minor chips on their fragile edges. I knew "less-than-perfect" was typically a huge turn-off for successful eBay sales. My lack of pottery knowledge to judge whether these pieces were worth the ten dollars asking price also held me back. These were big considerations for me at this time as my husband had just lost his job and that last ten dollars in my wallet wasn't ear marked for a risky garage sale bargain!

While the seller admitted she might be "giving away the farm" with this sale, she opted to put a low price tag on the set as there just wasn't time for any research due to her upcoming moving. She just wanted it gone.

My insecurity about my lack of knowledge of Majolica was overpowering my decision to part with the last ten dollars we had until the next unemployment check arrived! A stronger gut feeling crushed my hesitation and due to the quality and selection of other merchandise offered at this sale, impulse forced my "hunch" purchase. All the other items were of equal high quality and to my otherwise untrained eye were authentic ages for antique items.

After hesitantly parting with my last ten dollar bill, I watched the sale host tenderly and protectively wrap my splurge Majolica collection in bubble wrap.

Once home, I furtively researched this form of pottery and convinced myself it was worth the time and effort to list them for sale. Upon further inspection, I was pleasantly surprised to discover there appeared to be two different "sets" among the pieces and divided them up accordingly into two separate auctions.

Once listed, I watched my seven day auctions like a hawk. Early bids were encouraging for a home run! It wasn't until that last minute flurry of action that my fears were silenced. My hunch had paid off handsomely! The final combined selling price for the two sets was a whopping $1,400.00! One set sold for $900.00, the other for $500.00.

What I had purchased for ten dollars was indeed antique Majolica! Those minor chips I worried about as *flaws* were actually thought to be acceptable in these early pieces. I learned that the chipping of the delicately thin and fragile pointed ends of these items was common and usually found mostly on early examples of Majolica.

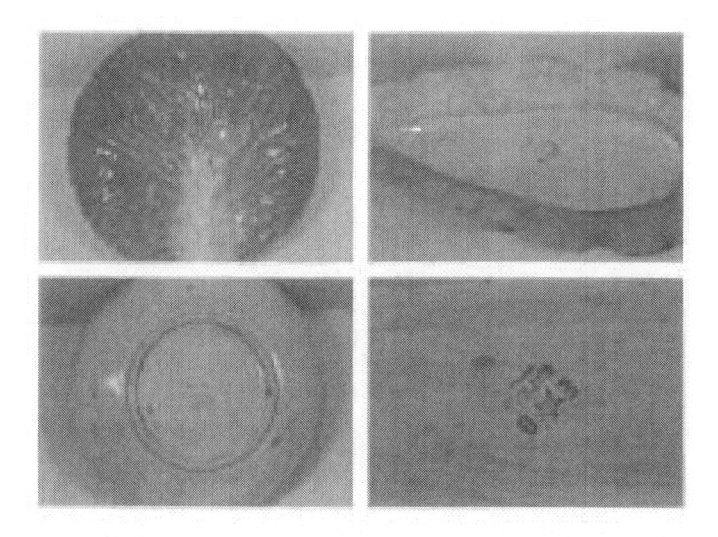

Remember, when your "eye" is drawn to it and your "heart" speaks, listen! Time is truly of the essence. If you walk away to consider a purchase someone else could be observing *your* interest and decide this might be something worth *their* grabbing. Or they might know the value and just wait for you to set it down so they can swoop in, pick it up and purchase it.

Golden rule for picking: If something speaks to you, pick it up and walk around with it until you are CERTAIN that you do or do not want it. You may not get another chance. Someone else may have their eye on it. And the converse applies as well. Watch others. If they consider something but later put it down it's your turn to own it. You may be able to snag an item you weren't certain about but later learned its value just by watching the shopping habits of others.

That $1,390.00 USD profit not only helped us during a tough financial time but also boosted my confidence in following my gut reaction when picking. It seldom lets me down!

Small Silvers

Estate sales are great alternatives for work days when you just feel like "playing hooky!" One such "cough-cough" *sick day* found me enjoying this privilege. In the "smalls" (which is a name for the small, valuable objects it contained) glass-covered cabinet was a one inch by one inch silver box that "spoke" to me. I asked the attendant to take it from the case for me to inspect. I asked if he knew what it was (I'm not afraid to show my ignorance, that's how I learn). He said he didn't know but perhaps it was a match box. The asking price was fifty dollars. When I asked if it was sterling silver, his reply was: "If it was sterling silver, it would be a lot more than fifty dollars!" Returning the item to him, I left empty-handed. Fifty dollars was a lot of money for something that spoke to my "eye" and heart but about which I knew nothing. The decision to walk away from that small silver box, gnawed at my conscience over the next few hours.

I left that sale and continued my *sick day* adventures to my next stop, an antiques shop. Often I'll browse through antiques shops to "study." Many items are tagged and identify the piece. Sometimes if you want to know more about an item, a store attendant is happy to share their knowledge with the hopes of a sale.

Immediately inside the front door of this small antiques shop I spotted a shelf loaded with books on antiques. I told you I'm a sucker for reference books! They are gold mines of information which provide me with lots of leisure time reading pleasure. Standing out as if it was placed there for my eyes only was a book titled, <u>Antique Small Silvers.</u>

Are you kidding me? I grabbed that book so quickly I was almost afraid someone would think I was stealing it! It was chock-full of pictures and descriptions of small antique items made out of silver! I could not believe my eyes; I was led to this store, THIS BOOK. After a quick glance through it, I didn't even try to haggle down the price and gladly paid the twelve dollars asking price and made a beeline for my car.

Feeling much like a successful thief who had gotten away with a heist, I spent the next several minutes just sitting behind the steering wheel of my car before even turning it on. I devoured this book at quickly as I could for anything that looked even remotely similar to that little silver box that I'd just walked away from at the estate sale and that was *still* on my mind. And then - I FOUND IT!

Immediately, I called my husband (this was before smart phones) and confessed my *sick day* activities. He did a quick internet search. Yep, there it was, a similar antique *vinaigrette* worth *at least* the fifty dollars asking price plus some room for a nice profit.

Queen Bee me, hightailed it back to the sale and bargained a thirty dollars purchase price. It was MINE! And no, I did not let on that I had identified it as *vinaigrette* in my new book and that it was *not* a match box as the sale promoter had earlier identified it.

Once home with my prized possession I did further online research and discovered a vinaigrette collector's group. Behind anonymity of online communication I shot off a quick email inquiry and a photo for some help in identifying my purchase. Note to self: Get over your hesitation asking the experts, some of them DO enjoy sharing their knowledge.

Later that night, my husband cleaned up the silver piece and made quite an exciting discovery. Years of aging had covered up four different *sterling silver* marks! What a beauty she was, from the 1800s and from Europe.

I soon received information from a gracious, new, online connection from the collectors group. What we had was not the vinaigrette that I thought my quick illustration research had matched, but in fact, it was an antique nutmeg grater! The now properly identified and cleaned nutmeg grater was listed on eBay and sold for over three hundred thirty dollars! The item could have realized a higher price but ours was minus the actual grinding mechanism.
While we certainly realized a great profit, of equal value was an educational and fun "antiques adventure" as well as new network

connections in our virtual Rolodex. I got over my affliction and the Cheshire cat went to work the next day feeling so much better!

That, my friends, is what drives my picking passion! It's not about the destination, but the journey.

The first picture is the one that I found. The second picture is one with a grater.

Carnival Glass

One of my early antique and collectible studies was carnival glass. For me, it was easy to recognize and identify in the volumes of collector's books in my library. There was also an abundance of examples to study available at resale shops and local sales. Low prices allowed adding to a collection with little investment. With a lot of pictures to study and examples to hold and learn from, it became fairly easy to match pattern pictures. This created a comfortable early learning process for my amateur eye.

I had been successful with early online sales of many different colors, patterns and makers of carnival glass. Each sale boosted my confidence in the ability to accurately identify patterns, makers and originals versus reproductions. Thus, I was able to recognize more difficult-to-find pieces while picking. The result became increased profits from my auction sales. Some of the more rare designs continue to maintain a solid retail profit today.

In 2010, shortly after buying our home that I used as home base for my "real job" in rural northern Michigan, I attended a farmhouse outdoor estate auction. Arriving early in the morning I walked around the two acre auction venue checking the various items going under the gavel that day. Initially, nothing really caught my eye although I did spot a few interesting things, should the price deem profitable.
As the auction proceeded, many items I had identified as potential purchases sold beyond my limit. Once the bidding passes my pre-set price limit, I'm out.

Although one might get discouraged by the lack of early wins, practicing patience can pay off handsomely. Unknown to me, the best was yet to come that day! When lots turned to items of no interest to me I engaged another auction strategy. I simply observed. I turned to watching other buyers to learn more about my competition.

On this day I was able to identify dealers, collectors and neighbors, as well as watch their bidding and purchase habits. Many had dropped out by this time, due either to having spent their allowance, time commitments or disinterest in remaining lots. My time, removed from the call of the barker, afforded me an opportunity to step back from the action and walk the grounds alone and take second and third looks at lots I may have given a mere glance previously in the day.

That's when I spotted *her*; a drop-dead gorgeous ice blue carnival glass plate. A rare beauty! There *she* was in all *her* glory, sitting among "commoners" in a "cheap" carnival glass lot.

I immediately recalled a recent article that one of the highest prices ever realized for carnival glass on eBay was for a piece of antique ice blue carnival glass. *She* was dazzling in sparkling ice crystals from a frosty autumn evening sleep atop the cold and splintered wood planks of the flatbed trailer turned glassware-display-table. I glanced around for peering competition. I put on my poker face and began checking off my mental carnival glass checklist. Could I discreetly pick *her* up and inspect *her* in quiet solitude? With swiftness and stealth acuity I did so and ran my fingers over *her* fragile old pointed edges.

Ice blue? Check. Brilliant iridescent carnival glass? Check. Uneven bottom? Check. No maker's back stamp? Noted. (Earlier pieces were often not marked). "Peacock on Fence" pattern? Identified. Every single delicate pointed edge in original condition, checked to perfection. No chips or cracks? Check. No mold seam lines? Check. Random straw marks impressed in the glass? Check. OMG! Could I be looking at a VERY RARE piece of ice blue carnival glass? Was I holding this gorgeous piece of glassware, MY glassware for a first time? I tenderly returned *her* back in *her* resting spot.

I stepped back from my newly coveted heart's desire with hands shaking but a forced stone-faced affect. Concealing my nervous excitement, I made a casual, inconspicuous walk back to the edge of the crowd to consult my "expert," eBay sold listings. While waiting for the lot to come up, I entered "ice blue; carnival glass; dish; peacock and fence" into a completed sales search on the eBay app on my phone. Several "solds" populated my search. I silenced a gasp as

I was dumbfounded at the final selling price of a similar piece. One had just sold for SIX HUNDRED DOLLARS! I anticipated perhaps a future four hundred dollars eBay sale, should I be lucky enough to win this item. I made an immediate mental note and set my auction purchase price limit at two hundred dollars for *her*. I would be happy to double my money.

That plate was GOING to be mine!

Standing in the freezing cold for five long hours keeping watch from a distance on my prized possession, I feigned interest in the ongoing auction. Every time a curious bidder would go near *her* and pick *her* up for inspection, my heart sank. "Don't you dare drop that thing and damage MY next huge eBay sale," I screamed silently over and over in my head during that long wait. "Get your hands off of MY *baby*!"

I prayed that my strategy to be patient, lay low and pay no more than two hundred dollars for that gorgeous piece of early and RARE carnival glass would pay off. If I realized the same six hundred dollar sale as the listing that I had confirmed on eBay, I would triple my money. Four hundred dollars would still be a nice profit.

I paced the grounds *all* day, drinking countless cups of coffee and watching with pleasure as many of the big shooters reached their financial limits and left early. They were dropping out before the action made it to the back lot where *she* patiently laid in waiting.

By the time that *her* lot came up, the crowd had dwindled to about fifteen survivors, down from original two hundred or so bidders, early on. I continued to scope out my competition. It appeared as though there might be one other bidder who had also been keeping an eye on the same carnival glass lot. By watching her from afar throughout the day, I surmised that she might be buying for resale as well. She had purchased a fair number of less expensive glass box-lots, likely to stock either a brick and mortar or online store. Finally, the auction made its way to the glassware filled flatbed. My hunch proved spot on! I put my game face on while struggling to control my emotions and caffeinated, nervous hands. I had waited all day. It was finally show time! I was going to have to fight for this. It was just her and me. Let the bidding begin.

"Choice out, carnival glass," barked the auctioneer. The highest bidder would get first choice of all of the carnival glass pieces on the flat bed. "Buy one piece, or buy them all, high bidder's choice." There were nine pieces. My limit, two hundred dollars and I only wanted ONE piece!

I accepted the auctioneer's opening bid at $5.00. "Yep!"
Then she bid $6.00.
"Seven dollars?"
"Yep," was my counter!
Then she took it up to $8.00 with the next incremental suggestion. I'm thinking, "Oh great, here she goes. I wonder where she has set *her* limit?"
"$9.00?" barked the auctioneer.
"Yep" and my nod affirmed willingness to take her up another dollar! "Ten dollars?"
Silence - Silence - Silence
"Going once, going twice, SOLD! $9.00" as he pointed the golden gavel in my direction.
The slam of the hammer proclaimed me to be the victor! It sealed my winning bid. I exhaled an exuberant, yet silent Amen. I am sure the sound of my heartbeat was just as loud as that glorious hammer knock.

"Lady, how many would you like?"
With a trembling voice I responded, "Three, please. I'll take three. This one," while CAREFULLY picking up my *newborn*, "I'll take this one," selecting another item and not even knowing why, "and I'll take this one." Again, why? I'm asking myself.
Apparently I wanted to continue my charade to make sure no one caught onto my game, although it really didn't matter now.

I walked one last time from the path that I had worn bare while observing my *baby* all day. I cradled *her* tenderly while hurrying to pay my whopping twenty-seven dollar tab; I couldn't get to my car fast enough! Deftly, my baby was swaddled into blankets of bubble

67

wrap that I'd brought in anticipation of such an event. After wrapping my other items I sat in the car in disbelief. I had literally snagged this rare gem for NINE DOLLARS!

I think I exhaled for the first time in hours. I relaxed for the first time since spotting *her*.

The next several weeks were spent doing a LOT of online research to be one-hundred percent positive in my identification of this piece.

68

I took pictures, wrote an accurate title and description and listed *her* for auction with an opening bid of my target, four hundred dollars, the price I would have been comfortable selling it for. Almost instantly, I had an opening bid. As the week of the seven-day auction progressed I got excited each time another hopeful bidder nudged up the selling price. At that last moment, as is typical of many eBay auctions, the frenzy began. Final hammer price, **$699.00 USD!** My nine dollars, patience, education and sweat equity garnered me enough money to pay for another ticket to Germany! Auf Wiedersehen!

My "finds" stories are not uncommon in the picking world. There are a lot of people who do this for a living, as I hope to do some day. Professional pickers have experiences like this frequently, I would imagine. When family and friends become aware of your talent they will start asking you to keep an eye out for things for them. And then they tell someone who tells someone. This is how a picker advances a career. In fact, this picker, with the help of friends and relatives, has turned a passion into a retirement transition career.

Should you desire, you also can do this! With taking that first step and going to sales and auctions, your journey begins. Keeping your eyes and ears open helps you learn a lot about this fun "sport." We all start somewhere; all it takes is that first step.

Look on craigslist, auctionzip.com or estatesales.net for sales near you. Check out a great garage sale app, "Yard Sale Treasures" for real-time sales that link to Craigslist ads to navigate local sales. This app is complete with a tool that will lead you from sale to sale using your smart phone, without having to use a separate GPS. There are countless new local online purchase opportunities popping up all the time.

Let this weekend be your inaugural event!

There is no single book you can read, nor one class you can attend that will compare to the education you get by going out into the masses and joining the fun. You will make a few mistakes, but that's the price of learning. One thing is for sure, there is never a lack of opportunity for learning in this field!

Lessons learned

- Know your product
- Know your competition
- Respect your competition
- Be patient
- Set a spending limit
- Know when to walk away
- Know your resale audience
- Have fun

PICKING UNLIMITED

The possibilities for places to find items for resale are endless. I am on constant lookout for opportunities to nab a bargain that has resale potential. You may see advertisements for wholesale and liquidation distributors who suggest that they have the best and largest inventories of the "hottest" items at the lowest price. I say look around you. What speaks to you may be just the thing that someone is searching for. Ask your kids or grandkids! They are a wealth of knowledge when it comes to the latest, greatest and hottest gadgets, especially when you're a generation or two removed from potential profits. Watch the advertisements on children's television shows. Moms of tots will do just about anything to snag the current "hot" toy. Think Cabbage Patch, Beanie Babies, Transformers, Hatchimals and this year's impossible-to-find toy, Fingerlings.

Start within the four walls of **your own home**. You hung onto that old toy or old butter dish from Aunt Martha because it struck a sentimental chord in your soul. If you're ready to part with it, there is probably a buyer who has been looking for one just like it! Emotion sells!

Beside items in my own home, I have also been known to make a profit selling some **gifts** I've received. I have only a couple of sentimental collections. Memories are my most-prized possessions and those don't sit on a shelf collecting dust. Therefore, it's easy for me to part with objects I find along the way. I do, however, have a deep respect and gratitude for people who find comfort in their "things." I realize profits from these collectors.

That's not to say that I don't have a lot of "stuff" sitting around. Remember, I'm a picker! I cannot pass up any items I can get for a great price and realize potential resale value. To make my point, I have several shelves full of such items just waiting to be listed on online resale markets or sold for a profit at my local flea market or garage sale.

A fun share is my story of a sibling-rivalry-turned-temporary-collector of Hall teapots.

It began with a fun oversized tea cup and saucer find at a sale. I paired them with an antique embroidered hankie for a "Goodbye Winter - Come on Spring" table centerpiece. When I placed it in the center of our dining room table, childhood memories took me back to a cobalt blue Hall teapot that my Mom always used when she would invite friends over for tea. I thought that teapot would complete the look of my centerpiece when paired with the oversized cups and saucers I had found.

I contacted my sister to see if she knew whatever happened to the original teapot. Yes, she had it. However, she wasn't willing to part with it. So, I turned to eBay to find one of my own. I wasn't looking to replace the teapot for a sentimental connection but only to complete a pretty table centerpiece. I did in fact find an exact match quite easily. It didn't wrap me in warm fuzzies like the original thick blue and gold Hall teapot that I remembered from my youth, but that wasn't why I wanted it. It paired well with my cups and saucers and complemented a delightfully inviting spring table décor.

My eBay search yielded exactly what I was looking for, and many more. One-by-one my Hall teapots multiplied. Each new addition to my collection intensified a desire to find every color, pattern and mold design available. At one point I had 25 beautiful examples of the Hall teapot line perched proudly on the dining room shelves built specifically to display them.

Family and friends also started giving me other teapots for my "collection." I had teapots of all sizes, shapes, designs and colors. I had become a "teapot collector" of something to which I really held no emotional attachment. My sibling rivalry had morphed into a compulsion to have a complete set of every Hall teapot ever made!!!

Soon, along came grandchildren with whom I developed a passion to share tea party time. Our ritual includes making cookies, letting one of the grandkids select a teapot to use each time, and then sharing our cookies with a pot of tea. As we "pip, pip, cheerio" with our pinkies in the air, we spend special time together.

The "lucky child of the day" gets to decide which teapot to use. Repeatedly, the chosen teapot was not one from my growing Hall teapot collection, or the coveted blue and gold Philadelphia style Hall teapot. It was a Disney teapot with a butterfly perched atop and Alice in Wonderland painted on the side that I received as a gift from our children during their visit to Disney World - because I collected teapots!

Sometime later I conceded that the Hall teapot collection didn't hold any emotion attachment or connection with my grandchildren. The teapots were simply collecting dust. I finally acknowledged that they were taking over shelf space that could be put to better use. Their purpose was fulfilled and I was ready to change the look of the dining room. So, I took all the teapots down except the blue one that started the madness. The other teapots have since been adopted by new collectors.

While preparing our setting for a recent tea party, I asked my granddaughter which teapot we were going to use. Without hesitation she blurted out, "Alice." Then she turned around and looked at the teapot wall. "Hey, Oma, where did all of the teapots go?" She had just realized that the lone survivors were Alice and Old Blue!

All is well. Their favorite to fight over some day, maintains a proud and safe spot in my glass cabinet! The shelves now hold my new and growing Roseville pottery collection.

With my "emotional emptiness" sated, it was now time to let someone else find comfort in the unique look and feel that only a Hall teapot can provide! I almost became a "collector" but was saved by a personality trait that yearns for change.

As you can see from my example of the teapot "dust collectors" in my home, your own home can be a treasure trove of stock to begin reselling. If you loved it, even if only for a time, someone else might just be yearning to add it to their collection! It may be time to exchange it for cash.

Garbage Picking

Yes, that's right, free trash. I am not ashamed to say that my husband and I have picked up many items sitting at the curb on garbage pick-up day over the years. Unashamed, we have crept along our city's streets in search of treasures left at the curb on trash day, much to the chagrin of our children.

The car would slow whenever Dad spotted a good "pick", sending our thoroughly embarrassed children ducking down in the back seat so their friends wouldn't see them! Years later as adults, however, I've heard them claim victory over an occasional pick that they had rescued! Making the parents proud!

Whenever possible, items reclaimed from the curb had new life breathed into them and became our household essentials. "New" dining room furniture, refurbished vacuum cleaners, lawn mowers or lawn furniture saw years more use. Many items were simply cleaned up and often resold for profit! As I write this we have a floor scrubber in the garage awaiting a new hose. Once fixed, it will go in our next garage sale. Thank you neighbor!

This innate ability to recognize gold in a trash heap is deeply rooted in my husband's DNA. Valuable repair skills were learned at the hand of his Depression-era father. He would salvage just about anything and restore even the most rugged cast-off to near-original factory condition and functionality. He not only taught my husband how to repair household items but later this ability served my husband as the foundation for a career as a skilled journeyman repair tradesman in the machine industry. Senior would dissect items for parts, clean and catalog them, and stow for future rework projects. My husband has many of the same catalogued drawers full of nuts, bolts, screws, springs, etc. There's always that one special piece close at hand when it's needed for a repair job,

My husband has also passed down the "art of repair" to our Generation X sons. While living in a disposable world they too have learned the value of and ability to, rescue and restore. The current societal norm to "pitch and replace" is defeated by "repair and reuse" as troubleshooting and restoration skills trickle down to a third generation in our family. We all pocket the cost of replacement and trade the savings to add to the coffer for the next travel adventure.

We feel that with the abandonment of respect for skilled trades in the American society today, it is beholden to those who possess those skills to pass them on. At my urging, my husband is contemplating offering a hands-on workshop where both young and old can bring a project that they wish to disassemble, clean and repair. I mentioned this to my friend recently and she immediately wanted to enroll her sons! Calling a repairman is expensive, not to mention a responsible environmental footprint that restoration offers.

The lesson here: There is money to be made when you cast your pride to the curb and exchange it for your neighbor's recyclables!

Resale Shops

"Thrifting" at resale stores has recently become vogue and is a lifestyle for many. Thrift stores, resale and consignment shops are quickly replacing big box retail establishments as the "go-to" shopping establishment for just about everything!

Thanks to someone else's generous donation, young and old alike are appreciating the value and selection of items that can be purchased second hand. Many use resale venues for their personal use simply to find unique items that are not available elsewhere. Some scour the racks for discontinued, antique or vintage items for both personal and resale purposes. Many resellers use resale shops as their sourcing (purchase to resell) outlet for inventory. With this insight you may now be able to spot resellers by simply watching shopping habits the next time you go to a resale or thrift store.

Secondhand retail establishments are packed with "flippers" (buy new or used at a low price to resell for a profit) resellers. Some are stealth in their approach; others are out right brazen in their rummage.

The sleuth and advanced reseller relies on personal knowledge, industry trends, or pure gut instinct. You may see some pick through racks of merchandise and/or glance at items on shelves; others eyeball items and simply add them to their carts. Some will openly scan UPC, ISBN or other codes and information to check real-time selling prices online and in brick and mortar market places. This is the strategy that I alluded to earlier.

These shoppers scan for potential resale value of items using phone applications that show recent sold prices in online marketplaces. Using this technique, a calculation for potential profit can be made instantaneously between the tagged price and a current sold value. A reseller then quickly decides whether or not the potential profit is worth the purchase and makes the "buy/don't buy" decision. There are many phone apps that offer this online barcode scanning resource. Checking eBay "sold" items or Amazon ranking can be done real-time as well and is often used as the gold standard for resale profit expectations.

As a result of thrift stores becoming aware of the influx of retail arbitrage in their stores, in many, prices have increased over the past few years to increase their profits. Many second hand stores now employ staff to check prices and mark inventory according to recent sold prices online, just as the reseller does. Due to this, in many instances raising the prices to deter retail arbitrage is trending and resulting in an opposite effect that occasionally finds the "thrift" store prices higher than new. In some instances large retail thrift store chains have run into significant financial difficulties by pricing themselves out of the resale price range and forcing resellers to alternative venues. Neither buyer nor seller wins when donations remain unsold on bulging stores racks and shelves.

Resale shop owners have mixed responses to shoppers purchasing for resale. Some embrace it, others despise the practice. They don't like the idea that someone is realizing profit on their price model. Some halt the activity once it is observed. Others befriend frequent buyers and even offer special privileges of reward cards based on volume purchasing. Some even offer "back room" stock selection privileges before the items even hit the sales floor. Some even hire the shoppers who later become employees!

My personal opinion is that resellers have brought a lot of profit to these stores that received their stock, usually from charity donations. Without the current heavy sales from resellers many thrift stores would not be realizing the huge boom to their businesses. If you think about it, that is exactly what every single retail establishment does, buy low to sell for a profit.

There are still opportunities to find niche category hidden treasures in the resale market. Higher profit and more commonly recognizable brand-name items are usually the items targeted most frequently for high prices in these stores. Lesser-known high-end clothing brands and obscure collectibles that fill every imaginable collecting category are occasional diamonds in the rough. A knowledgeable shopper could potentially realize a big profit from these lesser-known treasures in the resale world.

Flea markets in Europe

European flea markets – where Fleahopper was born – the inspiration for this book!

As mentioned earlier, my daughter's move to Germany was the spark that lit my passion for international flea market travel. That event, along with my desire to share my experiences with others, created a deeper passion to invite others during these trips to "come and play" with me. My hope through this book is to share the notion that international thrifting adventures truly can become a reality for anyone with the desire to pursue it.

From that serendipitous first event originally intended as simply a sightseeing trip to learn more about the new city that Heidi calls home, grew my passion for international flea market travel. From that single event emerged a new way for my daughter and me to spend some amazing times together. It was to become a new way to share experiences that I never, ever would have envisioned for us were it not for her move.

Each subsequent visit has included flea markets. We originally ventured only to nearby small villages and then to bigger local Bavarian flea markets. We advanced to road trips in neighboring Bavarian states, then countries and eventually created vacations with itineraries built specifically around seasonal flea markets throughout Europe. Each time we used her home as our base.

Since that first visit in 2001, I have been privileged to visit international flea markets in Germany; the Czech Republic; France; Switzerland; Austria; Denmark; Spain; Italy and the Netherlands. I continue to attend many in the United States as well. I'm not done yet!

Whenever possible, my husband and I travel together. We have met many wonderful people along the way who share our enthusiasm for this lifestyle and passion, and have been invited to stay with friends around the world.

South Africa, the UK and Ireland are just a few of the places for which we have standing invitations. Gracious friends have offered to host and act as tour guides. We cherish those friendships and invitations, which by the way, are reciprocated with the same offer from us. Flight paths are bidirectional!

www.fleahopper.com

FRIENDS - AROUND THE WORLD OR IN YOUR OWN BACK YARD

Our circle of rummaging compatriots spans the globe. Flea adventurers both near and far, became the foundation for building our priceless network of picking partners. Our web of relationships includes neighbors, international hosts, former exchange students, vendors, friends and friends-of-friends. Whether through chance encounter, formal introduction or strategic planning, each introduction has expanded our network and in some instances, created enduring friendships across the world.

It is impossible to share with you all the back stories that weave my web of international thrifting friends and colleagues. Following, are just a few examples of the miracle of friendships that I cherish, all created by allowing myself to open my eyes, ears and heart to a broader international circle of friends and opportunities.

Gerda

Remember the lady I referenced earlier who dubbed me "Chicken Scratch?" Her name is Gerda. Our chance meeting is a great example of how a mutual love of "junking" created a serendipitous opportunity and lifelong friend, the ultimate reward of networking.

While hopscotching between local garage sales in a northern Detroit suburb one Saturday morning a few years back, my husband and I stopped at a local sale. We overheard a private conversation between the two elderly women who were hosting the sale. I inquired about the price of an item for sale, "Wieviel? (how much is this)," I asked. That awkward feeble attempt to speak German began an enduring friendship with these sisters. We would learn that one sister lived in the home near ours that was hosting the sale; the other was visiting from the Black Forest area of Germany. Daring to step into their world via their native tongue sparked our connection. An instant bond was forged. A friendship blossomed.

As our friendship developed over the next several weeks, the eldest and German resident sister, Gerda, invited me to visit her home in the Black Forest area during my upcoming trip to visit Heidi. She offered to show me all of the "good spots" for thrifting near her home and neighboring Switzerland. I quickly learned that she, too, loves flea markets and resale shops and frequents them often. I jumped at her invitation. Several weeks later, after Gerda had returned home and I was visiting Heidi, we took off on a road trip from Bavaria to the Black Forest!

Not only did Gerda graciously host us with room and board, but also a delicious spread of food and a guided tour of her hometown area of Germany, the Black Forest. True to her promise, she guided us to stops in local resale shops as well as a couple of flea markets in bordering Switzerland.

As a bonus, we were joined by Gerda's friend, a true Swiss gypsy also named Heidi. She acted as our interpreter, price negotiator and tour guide in Switzerland.

We enjoyed an adventure beyond our wildest imaginations, free housing, amazing homemade local cuisine and a personal Black Forest flea market tour guide worthy of the highest five star rating. Gerda refused any compensation. She did graciously and humbly accept a hostess gift in exchange for her hospitality. I had brought her a beautiful Murano dish that she pined over at a Detroit area garage sale while visiting the US. I secretly purchased it and tucked it in my suitcase as a small token of thanks for her hospitality. To this day it sits on the sideboard in her living room in a quaint village near the Black Forest.

The discovery of secret spots, hole-in-the-wall resale shops and outdoor flea markets made this a grand picking adventure. My prime buy from this trip was an antique brown alligator purse for fifteen euros that sold for one hundred and fifty dollars upon my return home. Nice profit, awesome friends, great experience! The total cost of this road trip from my daughter's house was gas money to and from Bavaria and the Black Forest and the small cost of goods purchased. The value, priceless!

As of this writing Gerda is eighty-nine years old. She still attends flea markets and resale stores near her home. She doesn't travel internationally any more but we continue our friendship through emails and phone calls. She watches my eBay listings like a hawk!

Tom and Gabi

Tom and Gabi are local sports club teammates of my son-in-law. I initially met them through a casual, broken-English conversation at a dinner following a wrestling tournament. Tom, Gabi and I soon realized that in spite of our native language differences we shared a common language of "antiquing" and quickly learned to communicate thanks in part to Tom's command of the English language. Little did I know that our small talk that night would lead to, hands down, the most moving, real-life history lesson that I have ever experienced.

Tom grew up in the former communist East Germany. He spent his childhood climbing the hills of Ore Mountain bordering what is now the Czech Republic.

He told me stories of climbing castle ruins in hilltops that he claimed as his "back yard."

He would pretend that he was a knight fighting the enemy across the pencil-thin river separating his native communist backyard and the forbidden "Free Zone", just a single step across this narrow river.

During one of my first visits to Germany, Tom and Gabi invited me to join them for a road trip to his childhood hometown near Chemnitz, Germany. The purpose of their trip was to introduce their newborn baby to Tom's relatives as well as search for antique furniture to fill their historic barn home they were restoring. I nervously accepted the invitation from my new friends, agreeing to this first, solo, international journey without my daughter.

During our five hour drive across Germany, Tom shared memories of his many trips to and from his boyhood home in the former communist East Germany and his current exiled home in Bavaria. He shared with me one particularly life-changing trip, his recollection of his family's brave escape to freedom during his teen years.
As we drove along the autobahn, we approached a formidable reminder of former communist control, a Checkpoint Charlie. Tom recounted, with quiet reflection, the third and successful attempt of his family to seek freedom from the repression of communism. As we motored past the very spot where his family exiled into a new life when he was sixteen years old, Tom told me the story. He told of his father demanding that everyone in the car lay flat and to remain absolutely silent as they approached that stoic cold brick sentinel of captivity, or freedom, depending on which direction you were driving.

He went on to reflect that he was "not sure how long they drove along like that, but it seemed like forever." He was certain of one thing, the moment they had crossed from the life of suppression into a life of freedom. While still motoring in silence, Tom remembers the only signal that they had reached safety were the tears running down his father's cheeks. They were free! They had breached a life of communist rule and were breathing the fresh air of a new life. Life without money, without material possessions, but a life filled with the promise of freedom.

My friends THAT, is history come alive!

To this day, Tom's recall of the actual events of his family's day of emancipation gives me goose bumps, as well as a very deep appreciation for our American freedom. I will also never forget my own realization that day of how really unappreciative we can be for all that we take for granted.

During that whirlwind week we visited the industrial city of Chemnitz. The city is still crowded with soot-covered buildings, a reminder of ages of coal ash spewing from factories that sustained this communist area during those dark days.

Today this is a bustling, metropolitan Czech Republic border city and offers the usual retail shops, markets and restaurants found in most large cities. To those fortunate enough to have local connections there is also a plethora of small hidden specialty nooks.

Leaning on my friend's local heritage and shared love of treasure hunting I was allowed to share a local treasure trove of antiques picking at one such specialty nook. A discrete pole barn became temporary shelter to boxes of salvaged, newspaper-wrapped household goods abandoned by former East German refugees. Freedom seekers frantically fled their homes when the Wall went down in 1989. Before the last particles of brick dust had settled from the sudden and unexpected gateway to freedom, hopefuls ran to the border and left behind only footprints of their former lives and most of their worldly possessions. They left households full of "old" and ran with excited anticipation toward anything new. They were taking no chances that this opportunity for freedom was only temporary. Bland and colorless was traded for the breath of bright and colorful new lives.

During a recent conversation with Tom I recounted this visit. He told me that today (fifteen years after our shared visit) that this former pole barn without electricity is now a formal resale shop. The items are now well picked over and quite expensive. I'm so glad that our early visit remains my only memory of this former secret warehouse owned by twin brothers who saw value in salvaging the remnants of a generation of households and saving them from wrecking balls.

I couldn't bring myself to buy during this trip. I felt it my homage to respect those to whom the items formerly belonged; to honor their sacrifice, struggle and victory. I rejoice with them in their freedom.

Another unique picking stop during this trip was to Troedler Willi's, also in Chemnitz. Eccentricity whets your digging appetite before you even step foot in the door. It is a well-established, jam packed resale shop. Sharpen your eagle eye and plan to spend some time looking through the layers of vintage and antique goods. It's one of those places that can be quite overwhelming as you try to command your eye to focus on one area at a time. Alert - disorientation to time and space is common!

Several floors of everything from clothing to home goods, tools and architectural elements tempt your creative spirit and your wallet. The reminder of return flight airline baggage weights and fees keeps your spending prowess in check! I did walk out with an antique uranglas (Vaseline glass) pitcher with an annealed black handle for ninety euros that I was sure would yield a nice profit on eBay. Didn't happen! It was a European maker not well sought after in the US. Keep that in mind when picking abroad! It is now a piece in my mentor John's antique show offerings if you think you might just *have* to have it! I can probably still get my hands on it.

Sadly, I just learned of owner Willi's recent passing. His beloved shop is now permanently closed. I thank you Willi for the privilege of roaming among the treasures in your collection. The visual of your eclectic shop is etched in my memory forever. RIP Trodler Willi.

While Tom and Gabi stayed with relatives, I enjoyed my inaugural experience in a bed-and-breakfast in the tiny Saxon village of Hammerunterwiesenthal.

The "Guest House Pension Red House" is in the area of Germany known as the Erzgebirge, famous for metal work and wooden window candlesticks hand crafted by local artisans.

A short one block walk from my room, I crossed the German/Czech border via a narrow wooden foot bridge where an unattended border control shack still silently stands sentinel guarding friend and foe. This border separating Germany and the Czech Republic was the same pencil-thin river that forbade Tom's approach as a youth.

Over the course of my three day stay I freely crossed this tiny bridge between Germany and the Czech Republic.
Note that top photo is going into the Czech Republic and bottom photo is returning into Germany.

I thought often of my spoiled American privilege while crossing the bridge. My initial greedy selfish thought was of the angst that it must have wrought to those who yearned for the freedom to take that same single step as I did, the one that would plant them in that forbidden space and a life of freedom. Tom's response when I asked him if this ever crossed his mind as a child slapped me into self-inflicted shame. "I just knew I couldn't go over there," he replied, "so I just never thought about it!" If you are an American reading this, take a moment to think about this - don't we often want what we think we can't have! Not everyone expects that privilege!

Just across this now-friendly border is an austere open-air street market run by Vietnamese refugees. You can buy everything from black market alcohol and cigarettes to beautiful Czech porcelain, china and Christmas ornaments.

It is also home to a small restaurant that espouses to be the birthplace of the original Budweiser Beer.

92

Throughout the picturesque and heavily wooded area of old East Germany window sills are adorned with the aforementioned candle holders. This area is famous for not only these but a variety of hand crafted wooden items including baskets, lamp shades and miniatures. Many of the items are created specifically for Christmas. Cold harsh winters and abundant woods from the thick forests provide a perfect opportunity for creativity that also brings commerce to this small area of the globe.

I fell in love with the handmade crafts of the Erzgebirge area of Saxony in the small village of Gruhainichen. This is where I was first introduced to Wendt & Kuhn. This small village is home to the flagship shop where the artists carve and decorate woods from surrounding forests into intricate and delicate collectibles. Wendt & Kuhn are famously known for their collections of wooden angels. Each angel collection has differing and unique characteristics that collectors can identify.

I immediately fell in love with the angel collections. I was drawn toward the small enamel painted wooden angels with green wings and precisely eleven white dots painted on the wings of each one. Thus began my collection. Over the years my "band of angels" has grown. Each angel is playing a different musical instrument or is a member of the choir! I continue to be gifted frequently with new additions to my choir. They sing me a happy tune with every glance at my china cabinet and bring warm memories of not only the giver but my several trips to their homeland.

Here is a glimpse of half of my Wendt and Kuhn angel collection. It is the only collection with which I have an emotional attachment. Can you imagine why?

I could write an entire book about this trip alone. We have revisited this area several times and each time realized that there is still so much more to see, do and learn.

Tom and Gabi now have three beautiful daughters. They have fully restored their historic barn home and have filled it with many repurposed second hand shop and flea market furnishings. I visit with them frequently during my trips to Germany. It's always fun to catch up and hear about each other's newly thrifted finds. Our friendship flourishes.

Colette

I was referred to Colette serendipitously when looking for a B&B for King's Day during my first trip to Amsterdam. She is the owner and host of what I consider to be one of Amsterdam's most welcoming bed and breakfasts. She operates a quiet, warm and inviting B&B from her home in Landsmeer, Amsterdam. This Dutch village is a short ten-minute bus ride immediately across the Amstel River that shields you from the bustle and noise of often-rowdy revelers in the city center of Amsterdam.

I love the rooms in her cozy B&B. They are located on the upper floor of her home. The comfort of the beds, plentiful breakfast meals and the gracious, personalized service that she provides begins the moment she picks you up at the airport. She offers personalized tourist information and on-site purchase of tour tickets. If you are considering staying with Colette, keep in mind that you may also be saving on meals throughout the day. The aforementioned breakfast includes enough food to make sandwiches to pack for a bag lunch. Colette's rooms include potentially two meals in one, a safe stay and a comfy bed in a professional neighborhood village, all for one low price.

It remains one of our favorites place to stay in Amsterdam. We've returned several times.

Petra and Andi

Just darn good friends! Petra is Gabi's sister. Andi is my son-in-law's lifetime friend. Almost every time we visit Germany we are invited to their home. Petra and Andi entertain us with great company and always an amazing homemade Bavarian meal. No dinner is complete without a celebratory traditional shot of local schnapps. During my most recent trip this included learning about the "Allgaeu tequila shot" - slamming booze a new way!

The proper way to "do" this regional shot is to squirt a dab of Bavarian mustard on your hand, lick it and then throw back a shot of the biting local schnapps. You then "wash it down" with a small chunk of local sausage. Although hesitant to try, "in the name of friendship," I imbibed. Actually, it was quite tasty. The heat of Enzian warms all the way down - and then you relax.

One of my most memorable visits with Andi and Petra is from a few years ago when I was invited to "pick" the estate of Petra's late aunt before the contents of her lifelong home were to be offered for recycling. My decision-making skills were on overdrive this day. How much could I fit in my suitcase, space, weight and value-wise?

Oh, those baggage and customs limits control me every trip!

I fell in love with a large collection of vintage Easter dishes previously used by Petra's aunt. A cute Easter bunny and Easter egg design on sturdy ironstone pottery. I chose dessert plates, cups and saucers; service for six. They were carefully wrapped in bubble wrap and came to America in my carry on. I continue to use these every year. Not only have I created a tradition of serving Easter brunch on this set of dishware with our family, but each time we use it I am reminded of these special friends who allowed me the privilege of saving this fun holiday stoneware from the recycling center. It remains a fun table setting that my family looks forward to using each spring. And the bonus is that there are just enough to split between the grandkids when Easter brunch moves to their home in the future.

During this pick I also salvaged several World War II-era military items that belonged to Petra's uncle and some of her aunt's small jewelry items. My only regret at this opportunity was that I didn't have the knowledge for container shipment to the US. I could have easily filled a container and salvaged EVERYTHING in the apartment to save so many "good things" from being hauled off to the *wertstoffhof*!

Le-Anne

Le-Anne is my "second daughter" in Germany. She is a beautiful person with a big heart and a loving family. Le-Anne is originally from South Africa and is one of our daughter's closest friends in Germany. She is a founding member of my daughter's NESSie (Native English-Speaking Sisters) group.

NESSie is a local social group of expat women from around the world who have found each other in the Allgaeu area of Germany. Each member comes from a foreign country where English is the native language. They meet monthly to well, speak English! I join them when schedules coincide during my visits. No other language is allowed at their get-togethers other than English. I wish you could hear a snippet of all of the accents of one tongue! You would not believe how many dialects you can say the same thing in English!

Another tie that binds our friendship with Le-Anne is her love for resale purchasing and travel. She appreciates a good resale bargain just as we do. She welcomes us to visit her home each time we are in town. We always enjoy her extraordinary cuisine. We spend a lot of time talking, laughing and sharing life stories. We catch up on the latest resale shops open in the area and make sure to visit as many of them as we can.

It is also interesting to learn more about her native land each time we visit. She tantalizes us with travel tips to destinations near her childhood home of Cape Town, South Africa that include wildlife adventure and a ripe antiques industry. After learning about top adventure destinations from a local, who wouldn't want to visit warm foreign beaches, ride with wild animals and visit some of the finest antique markets in the world?

Cape Town, South Africa is now on our never-ending list of countries to visit. My husband and I have tentatively penciled in a late 2019 date to South Africa on our calendar. This will be welcomed timing to enjoy summer in SA and escape the cold of winter in the Midwestern, USA that time of year.

Home exchange travel experience is always reciprocal. As such we extended an open invitation to Le-Anne to visit our home in the United States. She ticked this dream trip off her bucket list in the spring of 2017.

During a whirlwind seventeen day visit we used our home in Berkley, Michigan as home base. We drove and drove and drove to show her not only our "Water Wonderland" state but neighboring states as well. She experienced an American road trip to rival none other. Our two-thousand mile road trip included visits to Chicago, Illinois and then up, down and across Michigan's upper and lower peninsulas.

Le-Anne learned American history at the fabulous theatrical production of "Hamilton" in Chicago. She enjoyed wine-tasting opportunities up and down Michigan's western coast and was thankful for this designated driver!

She donned her *swimming costume* (South African English for bathing suit) and dared to jump into the frigid early spring waters of Lake Michigan in the peninsular finger of Suttons Bay, Michigan. The visual of her daring icy plunge was so worth the price of a bottle of wine to us, her travel partners! I sure wish I could share the video in this book!

Le-Anne crossed the "Mighty Mac" bridge that joins Michigan's Lower Peninsula in Mackinaw City and the Upper Peninsula in St. Ignace. She visited the biggest Christmas store in America at Bronners in Frankenmuth, Michigan and added a few delicate baubles that made a successful journey home to adorn her Christmas tree in Bavaria.

At our vacation home in northern Michigan she relaxed and sipped coffee while watching the twisty Muskegon River flow lazily in front of her. She toasted marshmallows and made s'mores over an open fire and star-gazed in her pajamas. She learned all about American garage sales and fell in love with our neighborhood bargain-hunting culture.

Our offer to reciprocate her hospitality strengthened a friendship crossing many lands and cultures. We look forward to our shared visit to her native South Africa in 2019.

Anton and Sandy

At this Bavarian family farm you can earn a cow milking degree! Anton is Gabi and Petra's brother. Anton and Sandy own a local dairy farm, which also serves as a working Bed and Breakfast. If you stay at their B&B, you learn the life of a dairy farmer and work their farm along-side of them. Included is the usual lodging and meals, but you also share the responsibility of all chores related to tending their dairy cattle. Yes, this includes feeding, milking AND cleaning the barn. Be careful where you step!
Once you have successfully mastered the tasks, you earn your Cow Milking Diploma. It's a fun place to visit with wonderful people while learning first-hand the daily life of Bavarian dairy farmers.

C&C

When opportunity knocks, answer! That's exactly what my cousin and I did when we met this adventurous couple. C&C are related to my travel-buddy cousin, Stephanie. They are Home Exchange participants. They were privileged to participate in a Home Exchange with a couple from Valencia, Spain. C&C exchanged a year of living in this couple's home in Spain when the Valencian couple needed a place to call home for one year in the Oakland, California region during regatta season.

C&C extended the invitation to experience the local Spanish lifestyle to anyone wishing to stay in the apartment with them during their one year stay. That was all it took for Stephanie and I to consider a new-to-us, area of Europe. We booked our tickets to Valencia without hesitation.

This whirlwind ten-day adventure included: a tour through the LLadro Factory in Valencia, the BEST Sangria I've ever tasted (and never been able to replicate), a surprisingly urban impression of Spain, topless beaches, and one of the most vile and revolting flea market pick-pocket- distractions I've ever witnessed.

Tour book warnings of sly tactics employed by expert thieves do not lie. Though warned, I wasn't prepared for my disgust at the level to which someone would stoop to try to steal from us. I was stopped in my tracks when an elderly woman publicly fondled the genitals of a naked male newborn cradled in her arms; all to shock and distract so that her accomplices could pick your pockets! Fortunately, my pre-market-visitor knowledge of and attention to the recommendations of guarding my cross-body money pouch evaded their thievery. The "Beware of Pick-Pocket" signs surrounding this Valencian flea market area were not to be ignored!

Perhaps the highlight of this trip, however, was a side trip to Barcelona, the capital of the Catalan region that C&C insisted we take. Prior to our arrival in Spain C&C booked train tickets and a hotel reservation in Barcelona for Stephanie and me. They drove us to the train station and even prepared a bag lunch for us to enjoy during our two hour ride to Barcelona. The timing of our visit was perfect to witness a glimpse of Catalan history.

Our short stay happened to coincide with the annual remembrance of Catalan's loss of independence to and annexation by Spain. Locals who continue to mourn this event peacefully demonstrated through speeches, music, marches and local traditions. We were privileged to witness this. The dirge of the music in the streets and the somber mood of this day continues to move me with compassion for their loss and make me appreciate their hope and continued fight.

What a dichotomy of sights, sounds and emotions as well as an amazing yet unforgettable experience. This was *not* the Spain I had envisioned, but oh, so much more!

THE TIMES THEY ARE A CHANGIN'

This crazy lifestyle began when I thought my world was falling apart when our daughter moved across the ocean! Little did I know that a new lifestyle was about to unfold. It is now a part of who I am, who we are as a family and what we love to do. All is well with my soul. I am at peace with the distance between my daughter and me and grateful for the opportunities that it provides. I have adjusted to mothering and grand mothering from six thousand miles away. I look forward to any time we spend together. I always shed a tear when we say goodbye!

As our days in Corporate America wind down, the time constraints of limited "vacation days" will no longer restrict our datelines or our desire to tick more international flea market destinations off of our to-do list.

For those of you who are saying to yourself, "I can't afford this," we say that with a little extra work, determination, and planning, you can too! If this middle class family can do it, so can you! We are able to fund these opportunities through nothing more than part time online reselling efforts, determination and a burning desire for new adventure. Remember we use nothing more than our eBay profits to make it happen!

It is often as economical to make transatlantic trips as it is to vacation in America, sometimes even less expensive. Set your sights abroad. Global travel is no longer just for the rich and famous. It is a surprisingly affordable opportunity for those who are willing to embrace cultural diversity, grow a network of friends and business associates and stretch a vision to include international experiences.

Employ cost-cutting strategies for flights and housing; network before, during and after you travel; watch the magic unfold that will create opportunities for your future trips of a worldwide flea market-adventure lifestyle!

MY STEADFAST DREAM

Our dream is to travel frequently and continue to make friends around the world with folks who share this passion. We dream to make good on open invitations and welcome our international friends to experience their dream journeys to America as well. Unimaginable opportunities have forged one link at a time, a chain of priceless friendships that nurture with each visit. Never, in my wildest dreams could this middle class American gal have imagined this life filled with wonderful friends around the globe!

That blue, hardwood and leather train case won by my father when I was nine years old sparked a passion, and circumstance and opportunity fueled our "thrifting life." Lifestyle values instilled by depression-era parents root our expectations. We love the simple life and road less taken. We play out our story on a global platform. We continually seek new friends and opportunities and engage in thrifting conversations along the way. You really never know where that next connection may take you!

We have the horizon of retirement creeping upon us. This means we'll no longer be limited by the nine-to-five restrictions of Corporate America and will be able to enjoy the opportunity to freely explore wherever and whenever our adventurous lifestyle calls us. Continuing our international travel as well as exploring more picking spots in the US remains our goal as does continuing the lifelong learning that has brought us to this point.

We have serendipitously enrolled in the School of International Flea Marketing and love the possibilities for never-ending continuing education! We have learned that there is no terminal degree in this educational tract. There are now more reasons than ever to employ strategies to stay relevant in the reselling arena as we keep our eyes open for that next unique *"something"* while picking and debate which profit may pay for our next trip. Now that's the stuff that dreams are made of!

This lifestyle may not be for you. If it is for you, perhaps not such a grand scale. That's OK. Use our story and any of the lessons learned along the way to inspire a vision and create your own journey. Start with baby steps. Again, as my dad always said, "Put one foot in front of the other and one step at a time you will get there."

Our suggestion for you is to start small but dream big. Keep your eyes open, ears alert and heart receptive for even the smallest voice that may speak to you. Trust the instinct that says, "I too *can* do this!" Above all else, enjoy the journey as much as the destination.

Gather those lemons that life throws at you. Squeeze the textured peels until the flow of bitter juices changes to sweet nectar of thirst-quenching lemonade of opportunity. Embrace that rock in the bumpy road of life meant to dissuade you. Use it as the first stone upon which you build a strong foundation for a life you never thought possible. And sometimes, the surprise that unfolds before you is a life beyond your wildest imagination.

AN OPEN INVITATION

"Traveling on the cheap" is a conversation I would love to share with anyone who may be interested in going on a European flea market adventure. My dream is to gather like-minded travelers to join us for an international picking journey. If that person is you, please get in touch. Perhaps with a "first time" guided tour you, too, might catch the travel picking "bug" and begin a new chapter in your autobiography as an international flea market picker!

I will even share some of my favorite travel tips for cheap flights and upgrades to first class like this one that only cost me fourteen euros!

If that is you, please get in touch! Let's talk! I can be found via our website, www.fleahopper.com or you can send an email to fleahopperthrift@gmail.com. I'd love to connect and perhaps meet you along the road someday. If anything in this book has piqued your interest and you wish to learn more or if you have questions or would just like to chat, please get in touch.

Now you know how Fleahopper was born, works, plays and lives - hopping across the ocean to visit as many flea markets as one life is privileged to experience! We hope to cross paths with you in our travels. "Carpe diem"- seize the day!

Thank you for coming along for our ride. We hope that you have enjoyed our story and that it may inspire you to begin a new chapter in your own journey. The world is ours to travel. Enjoy your travels wherever your dreams may take you.

Made in the USA
Lexington, KY
20 February 2018